ONE STEP FROM GLORY

ONE STEP FROM GLORY

The Story of Tottenham Hotspur's
Champions League Campaign 2018/19

Alex Fynn and Martin Cloake

First published by Pitch Publishing, 2019

Pitch Publishing
A2 Yeoman Gate
Yeoman Way
Worthing
Sussex
BN13 3QZ
www.pitchpublishing.co.uk
info@pitchpublishing.co.uk

A CIP catalogue record is available for this book
from the British Library.

ISBN 978 1 78531 598 5

Typesetting and origination by Pitch Publishing

Printed and bound by TJ International Ltd

Contents

As a director of Saatchi & Saatchi, Alex Fynn helped create the first advertising campaign for a football club, for Tottenham Hotspur, back in the 1980s. He subsequently advised the FA, the Football League and several Premier League clubs on media and marketing. This is his fourth book on Spurs.

Martin Cloake has supported Spurs since the early 1970s and has travelled all over Britain and Europe to watch the team. A writer and editor, he has co-authored six previous books on the club, including two award-winning official publications.

Also by Alex Fynn

(with Lynton Guest) *The Secret Life of Football, Heroes & Villains, Out of Time*, and *For Love or Money*

(with H Davidson) *Dream On*

(with Olivia Blair) *The Great Divide*

(with Eric Cantona) *Cantona on Cantona*

(with Kevin Whitcher) *The Glorious Game, Arsènal: The Making of a Modern Superclub* and *Arsène and Arsenal*

Also by Martin Cloake

(with Adam Powley) *We Are Tottenham* and *The Boys from White Hart Lane* (with Adam Powley and Doug Cheeseman) *61: The Spurs Double, The Glory Glory Nights* and *The Lane*)

(with Alan Fisher) *A People's History of Tottenham Hotspur Football Club*

In memory of Ralph L. Finn,
Tony Fuller and Daniel Stern

Miss you most at times like this

Acknowledgements

IT WILL be obvious that this book could not have transpired without the help of many people, so first and foremost in the queue for thanks is Jane Camillin without whose enthusiastic backing there simply would not have been a book. So heartfelt thanks to her and to Katrina Law, Alan Fisher, Bernie Kingsley and David Stern, Spurs stalwarts who kindly read the manuscript, pointed out errors – any that remain are entirely our fault – and made suggestions, the majority of which were adopted to the benefit of the manuscript.

Grateful thanks are due to Duncan Olner for his eye-catching cover design, to Dean Rockett for his skilful copy-editing and to Graham Hales, typesetter *par excellent*. Greville Waterman was a constant source of support as was Rhoda Fynn, who compensated for her husband's lack of computer skills. The understanding of Cath Mackenzie, Danny and Tom Cloake was increasingly essential as deadlines drew near. Thanks are also due to Adam Powley and Michael Green, as they are to all the fans who have enriched the writers' matchday experience in a most momentous season.

Match reports from *The Telegraph*, *The Guardian*, *The Times* and *The Independent* provide the underlying theme so permission for their use was a prerequisite. So thanks for granting this to Ruth Marsh at *The Telegraph*, Nick Shackleford and Andrew Pulver at *The Guardian*, Bill Burrows and Miguel Delaney at *The Independent*, and Tim Hallissey, Robin Ashton and Marc Cutler at *The Times*. And to those reporters whose skill in producing 700-plus words of instant insight and analysis against such tight deadlines never ceases to amaze. So thanks to Sam Wallace and Matt Law (*The Telegraph*), Daniel Taylor and David Hytner (*The Guardian*), Miguel Delaney (*The Independent*), Henry Winter and Alyson Rudd (*The Times*).

The authors and publisher would like to thank © Getty Images for permission to reproduce the photographs in this book.

Introduction:
Memories are made of this

IN 1961 to commemorate Spurs' Double-winning season, Ralph L. Finn wrote *Spurs Supreme*, modestly sub-titled, 'A review of soccer's greatest ever side 1960-61'. It became former Spurs chairman Irving Scholar's favourite book. As he explained, 'it recorded every game played that season by way of re-printing at least one newspaper report. I must have read it at least 50 times over, never tiring of its content.'

Back then, very few matches were broadcast on black and white television (*Match of the Day*'s highlights first began in the London area on BBC2 in 1964). So match reports in the daily and Sunday newspapers supplemented by the occasional second half radio commentary and *Sports Report* on the BBC Light programme were the chief means of finding out in detail how your team fared. Today of course, all major matches are available instantly on pay television, internet and your phone, giving rise to immediate debate on Twitter, Instagram and radio phone-ins. The omnipresence of information notwithstanding, newspaper reports still provide an essential service for the football supporter: articulate, sometimes eloquent reporting and analysis viewed through an expert eye providing an authoritative and objective permanent record of key events.

Match reports taken from the *Telegraph*, *Guardian*, *Times* and *Independent* provide the narrative thread for *One Step from Glory*; a comprehensive account of Spurs' most successful season in European football's premier club competition.

'If we are not in Europe, we are nothing', said Bill Nicholson, the club's most successful manager. Spurs and Europe is an ongoing love affair encapsulated by those glory, glory nights at White Hart Lane under floodlights against continental opposition which has defined Spurs. And that love affair has been rekindled in earnest in 2019.

Of course, the last chapter could so easily have had a Hollywood ending but as Danny Blanchflower, the captain of Spurs' Double-winning side, memorably said, 'Football is not really about winning or goals or saves or supporters... it's about glory. It's about doing things in style, doing them with a flourish; it's about going out to beat the other lot, not waiting for them to die of boredom; it's about dreaming of the glory that the Double brought.' This is why the Spurs 2018/19 Champions League campaign – so unexpected, so unimaginable, the most improbable of dreams – touched the heart of every Tottenham Hotspur supporter and gave so much pleasure to the many millions of followers of the glory game.

1

The Spurs Way

THE SPURS Way is not the name of a road leading to the new stadium, but it is a route that will run through this story. It is central to the identity of Tottenham Hotspur FC and understanding it is the key to achieving any kind of success at Spurs.

One of the enduring attractions of the game is that, despite the increasing application of science, outcomes often defy rational analysis. The Spurs Way is a romantic concept in a hard-headed world and is part of what enables football to stay a sport, rather than a manifestation of statistics. As Danny Blanchflower, the captain of Tottenham Hotspur's 1961 Double-winning team, once said when asked who would win a match he was co-commentating on: 'I don't know, that's why they're playing the game.' If we know who is going to win, what is the attraction of watching? If the club that has the most money, that pays the highest wages, that accumulates what are statistically proven to be the best players is guaranteed victory, football is no longer a sport.

In the football business of 2018/19, Tottenham Hotspur's appearance in the Champions League Final was not meant to happen. And it caught the imagination for precisely that reason. It was the product of a remarkable revival in fortune, and of a rediscovery and redeployment of the Spurs Way. It signalled that, as the Spurs went marching on, the soul of football was not a-mouldering in the grave.

If you think there is a danger of overplaying the importance of character and identity to a football club, set Spurs aside for a moment and consider the fortunes of Manchester United under José Mourinho. One of the most successful managers of the modern era – the only one who has won the Champions League with three different clubs – Mourinho ultimately failed at Old Trafford for a number of reasons, among them, perhaps, because he did not understand or value the club's character. Manchester United lost their way, supporters and club lost their connection, players lost that extra bit of heart that comes from drawing on characteristics rooted deep in a club's DNA. Fanciful nonsense? In the end, it's a subjective judgement, but Spurs' European adventure in 2018/19 is the tale of a club rediscovering its sense of identity, reconnecting with a past – one which it is often criticised for clutching too closely to its heart – in order to create a new present and, maybe, a glorious future.

At Tottenham Hotspur, the demand for football played in a particular way runs deep. The Spurs Way is football played for the most part on the ground, with intelligence, where the creation of the end result is valued as much as the end result itself. It is often misinterpreted, most frequently by those who quote Blanchflower's famous maxim without fully understanding what the great man said. The game was about glory, for sure, but he went on pointedly to say, 'it's about going out to beat the other lot, not waiting for them to die of boredom'. Winning was as important a part of Danny's vision as style, and he came to Tottenham Hotspur because he saw in the club's modality an echo of his own.

Tottenham Hotspur's daring can be traced right back to the club's establishment by a group of schoolboys in 1882. They were in search of a sport to play during the winter months when the cricket season for their club was over. Enthralled by the tales of the knight who spurred his horse onto the battlefield in advance of the men he commanded and perhaps inspired by lines such as 'And if we live, we live to tread on kings', the boys named the club Hotspur after Sir Harry Hotspur, the real-life Sir Henry Percy who was turned into an iconic swashbuckling character by Shakespeare.

Tottenham Hotspur quickly developed an identity, as a team that carried the standard for the emerging suburbs of the age, for the largely amateur south against the professional might of the industrial north, and for playing entertaining football at odds with the traditional English game. Towards the end of the 19th century, the English game had relied on power and brawn to batter the opposition into submission. The pass and move method was regarded with some suspicion. Jonathan Wilson, in his history of football tactics, *Inverting the Pyramid*, talks of 'Englishmen convinced that anything other than charging directly at a target was suspiciously subtle and unmanly'. It was in Scotland, most notably at Queen's Park, that what was termed the combination game was honed, the forerunner of what would become push and run. One of the club's players, inside forward John Cameron, fetched up in North London in 1898 and his style of play fitted in with the ideas of Spurs' founding members who were keen for their team to play fast, attacking, entertaining football.

They certainly made people sit up and take notice. In 1901, as player-manager, Cameron led Spurs to victory in the FA Cup Final against Sheffield United in a contest that so captivated the public's imagination that over 100,000 people flocked to the Crystal Palace in South-East London. And to this day Spurs remain the only non-league side to win the FA Cup. The seeds of glory had been sown.

The work of the early pioneers such as Cameron earned Spurs the nickname 'the Flower of the South', and was advanced from 1912 onwards by Peter McWilliam. McWilliam was hugely influential, managing the club for 19 years in two periods between 1912 and 1942 and establishing a youth development system that sought to embed the Spurs style of play throughout the club.

McWilliam's system spawned two influential figures, Arthur Rowe and Bill Nicholson, who stayed at Spurs and made history. In 1949, Rowe, a Tottenham lad, returned to the club he had played for before the war to take charge after a long fallow period. He immediately restored character and purpose through deploying a modernised version of the passing game, reprising the tactics that had been developed in central Europe between the wars. This style of play emphasised short passing, forwards dropping deep to collect the ball, a fluidity that saw the switching of positions and a willingness to let the ball, rather than the physical strength of the players, do the work.

Rowe modestly denied he was a revolutionary; his inspiration was much more workaday. 'I merely evolved the idea after watching kids running down the street, flicking a tennis ball against a wall and collecting the instant rebound in full stride,' he said. 'The wall-pass, one-two touch play, push and run, call it what you will, we developed it at Tottenham from the rear, from the goalkeeper up to the front right through the team.' The tactics Rowe explained were based on 'accuracy. We had two or three great performers [he probably had in mind Alf Ramsey, Ron Burgess and Eddie Bailey], and we had a lot who were not but they were all made to look great players because of the system we adopted, and because they played in a winning side.' His axiom succinctly summed up his philosophy. 'Make it simple, make it accurate, make it quick.'

Rowe's team won the Second and First Division titles and finished runners-up in three successive seasons (1950–53), sending shock waves around an English game suffocating in its post-war insularity and arrogance. What is now recognised as the modern Spurs Way had been firmly established.

Push and run heralded a period of prowess unparalleled in Spurs' history, unfortunately seemingly over almost as soon as it began. As the manager kept faith with his ageing team, Spurs dropped down the table to 16th place before ill health forced Rowe's premature retirement in 1955. His assistant, Jimmy Anderson, replaced him.

Quality players such as Danny Blanchflower, Bobby Smith, Maurice Norman and Cliff Jones were added to the squad and Spurs' fortunes turned the corner until ill health again forced a change in the managerial seat. However, the seamless succession was maintained when Anderson's assistant, Bill Nicholson, replaced his boss in 1958. As with his two predecessors, Bill Nick was a Spurs man through and through, most notably as a tenacious wing-half member of Arthur Rowe's championship sides. His first match in charge, an astounding 10-4 victory at home to Everton, proved a false dawn and Spurs ended the season languishing in 18th place. The quip forward Tommy Harmer made to Bill Nick as the players left the pitch after the Everton game seemed to have taken on the character of a prophecy – 'It's downhill all the way now,' Harmer is reported to have said.

Bill Nick then made an unforeseen but ground-breaking decision: he built his hopes for the future around an ageing, attacking wing-half who had been dropped by Jimmy Anderson supposedly for taking the initiative and reorganising the team's tactics during a game when he believed circumstances warranted it. 'I told Danny', explained Anderson, 'it was no use my picking the team on Friday if he was going to change it on the field on Saturday.' Far from feeling undermined, Bill Nick was emboldened by Danny Blanchflower's singular approach. Asked how Northern Ireland reached the quarter-finals of the 1958 World Cup, Blanchflower explained their unexpected success was based on 'our new tactics: we equalise before the others have scored'.

With the acquisition of Bill Brown, Les Allen and John White and with Dave Mackay restored to full fitness (he had arrived from Hearts carrying an injury) the missing pieces of the jigsaw were in place and Blanchflower began to believe that Spurs could do the Double. 'I told some of the players that I thought we could do it. "Oh yes", they said, as if they did not believe it or maybe they didn't know what I was talking about,' said Blanchflower. 'Then I mentioned it to Bill Nick. He looked at me cautiously, as if it was another of my fancy ideas. Then he surprised me. "I was thinking about that myself," he said. We agreed that we all had to believe in it to do it. We must create the right atmosphere.'

After finishing two points behind Burnley in third place in 1960, the scene was set for an historic season.

Bill Nick's Double-winning side of 1960/61 is still described by many who saw it as the greatest of the 20th century. It captured the imagination not just by playing football the like of which had never been seen before and breaking record after record – most successive wins at the start of the season (11) in a 42-game First Division, most victories (31), most away wins (16), most goals in the club's history (115) – but by dint of being in the right place at the right time. As post-war austerity faded away it was replaced by the age of mass entertainment, of the leisure society, and Spurs were as much a show business hit as a footballing sensation.

Tottenham Hotspur not only played stylish football; for many fans and new converts to the game, they were stylish football. Spearheaded by the incomparable Jimmy Greaves, the latest in Bill Nick's astounding series of transfer coups, Spurs finished third in 1961/62, and second in 1962/63. Bill Nick went on to lead his men to the first victory in European competition by a British club. This was followed by another FA Cup in 1967 and, in the early 1970s, two League Cups and another European trophy, the UEFA Cup. He had fashioned Tottenham Hotspur into one of the most famous sides in Europe and helped ensure the club's name was synonymous with flair and excitement for generations to come.

When Bill Nick left in 1974, disillusioned with the way the game was going, Spurs lost their way. Constant battles with players who did not share his principles had worn him down. But while he knew he was no longer up for the job, he knew a man who was. Sad to say the Spurs directors did not see themselves as custodians of a special institution, that their role was to preserve the Spurs Way for future generations. Otherwise, how could they ignore Bill Nick's recommendation of Danny Blanchflower as his successor and select instead Terry

Neill, a former Arsenal captain? A crass appointment that was to be repeated 25 years later when Alan Sugar appointed George Graham as the Spurs manager.

Spurs fell into the old Second Division in 1977. The great entertainers were no more, and the club exuded the air of a music hall artist whose patter no longer connected with his audience. But it drew on its resources and propelled itself back to the top. In this instance the directors got it right. Rather than sack Keith Burkinshaw, the young manager who had been in charge when Spurs were relegated, they stuck by him. The captain, Steve Perryman, refused to leave the ship that had 'gone down on my watch' and his steely determination and football intelligence combined with the creativity of a gifted young midfielder called Glenn Hoddle were instrumental in taking Spurs back at the first attempt. Once again those inherent, essential ingredients were present – silk, steel and a willingness to draw on and develop what was already there.

The following year, Burkinshaw elevated the Spurs Way to new heights – signing two Argentinian World Cup winners, Osvaldo Ardiles and Ricardo Villa, for a combined total of £750,000. It is difficult to convey just what a sensation this was – in 1978 foreign stars didn't sign for English clubs, and World Cup winners certainly didn't join clubs that had only just been promoted. The transfer swoop catapulted the club back into the public eye. It was a bold, brash break with the past, a wind of change that would blow through English football.

The Argentinians took time to gel, but between 1980 and 1984, Tottenham Hotspur became one of the most successful, entertaining sides in the country. Hoddle, dubbed 'Ghod' by the fans, was the fulcrum of the team. On the way to lifting the UEFA Cup in 1984, he famously handed out a footballing lesson to the great Johan Cruyff himself when he came to White Hart Lane with Feyenoord towards the end of his playing career. Even so Hoddle was regarded with suspicion by England managers. Despite scoring with a 20-yard volley on his international debut he was promptly left out of the next match, manager Ron Greenwood justifying his decision by saying that 'Sometimes a player's weaknesses can be ignored, his strengths over-ride everything, but I did not feel this was the case with the young Hoddle.' Unsurprisingly, Danny Blanchflower had a different point of view. 'Hoddle a luxury?', he asked rhetorically. 'It's the bad players who are a luxury.'

Glenn Hoddle was adored by the fans because he was a creative, cultured and exciting player, the latest in a long line of his ilk such as Eddie Bailey, Tommy Harmer, Alf Ramsey, Blanchflower, Jimmy Greaves and Alan Gilzean. Inspired by Ghod, the FA Cup semi-final replay demolition of Wolverhampton Wanderers on a wild night at Highbury, of all places, in 1981 was, for many Spurs fans who witnessed it, akin to the spectacle raved about by those who witnessed the Double team. Football played the Spurs Way.

After Hoddle – who was integral to FA Cup wins in 1981 and 1982 and to David Pleat's 'nearly men' of 1987 (third in the league, League Cup semi-finalists and FA Cup finalists) who featured another great entertainer, Chris Waddle – came Gary Lineker, Paul Gascoigne, a new generation and another FA Cup win in 1991 under Terry Venables. Spurs were doing what they did, turning heads, turning on the style. But then it all went wrong.

From the moment he took over the club he loved in December 1982, Irving Scholar's *modus operandi* was to ensure that Spurs could continue to buy the sort of players he admired, who exemplified the Spurs Way. To that end, Tottenham Hotspur became the first football club to go to the Stock Exchange. Similarly, the onus was put on the expansion of commercial activities. Scholar was a football visionary, probably the first chairman to anticipate the potential of broadcasting, commercial and matchday revenues. Unfortunately, he moved too fast and too far for the times. And although his heart was undoubtedly in the right place, his hands-on approach caused problems on the playing side and his vision was not one universally embraced by supporters. Ironically, while the club's merchandising – replica shirts, videos, books and the like – was innovatory and profitable, the decision of the plc to diversify into non-football areas such as leisurewear was a drain on the football club. Instead of providing a war chest, it saddled the club with a mountain of debt forcing Scholar, after flirting with Robert Maxwell, to sell the love of his life to Alan Sugar.

Looking back, Tottenham Hotspur exemplified the 1980s. Everything looked fine on the surface, but the substance was lacking. Maybe eyes had been taken off the ball, but the reality was soon revealed to be very different from the flash exterior. Somewhere along the line, the bit in Blanchflower's quote about winning had been forgotten.

Spurs drifted, stabilised by new owner Alan Sugar after dismissing his erstwhile partner, Terry Venables, but becalmed, existing on history, some exciting individuals, and at times the sheer bloody-mindedness of the owner. Sugar was, and remains, a controversial figure. He faced the authorities down when they deducted points from his club and banned it from the FA Cup over financial irregularities he inherited from the previous regime. He brought in superstar Jürgen Klinsmann in a swoop reminiscent of the deal that brought Ossie and Ricky to White Hart Lane all those years before, and he sanctioned the signing of David Ginola, who brightened some dark days as the club continued to mark time.

Supporters weren't always convinced Alan Sugar really got the club and at times he seemed suspicious of much about the football business. He'd kept Spurs alive, but it was becoming hard for supporters to understand what for. When he eventually sold up, professing his despair with an ungrateful fan base but nonetheless still pocketing a tidy sum for his troubles, new owners ENIC and chairman Daniel Levy made a bold first move. They axed manager George Graham, unpopular not as much for his Arsenal connections as for the fact that the style of football he played was in almost direct opposition to the tenets of the Spurs Way, and installed

Ghod as the new manager. Opinion remains divided on whether ENIC were looking for an instant crowd-pleaser or had a deeper plan to restore the club's spirit. In his defence, Graham will point out he'd guided Spurs to their first trophy for eight years, the 1999 League Cup. And without resorting to all that Spurs Way malarkey.

Whatever the reasoning, the appointment of Hoddle – hailed by fan website *TopSpurs* as 'the return of sunshine football' – did not work out despite a promising start and he was sacked. ENIC trumpeted a series of grand plans involving continental management systems with directors of football, only to drop them when they went awry in favour of conventional English-style autocratic gaffers, then return to a more continental system… all the while affirming the necessity to develop young talent. The need to do so was evident as Spurs, one of the clubs who led the breakaway Premier League, had failed to capitalise on their own vision and had fallen far behind many of their rivals. As players came and went at an increasingly rapid rate, and with frequent changes of manager as well, fans began to question what their club had become and where it was heading.

The arrival of Martin Jol in 2004 brought Spurs some success and the fans some belief. Jol stepped up after another of ENIC's cunning plans fell apart when highly regarded former Lyon and France manager Jacques Santini walked out just 13 games into his tenure, disagreements with sporting director Frank Arnesen said to have prompted his decision. Caught unawares, the club had little option but to offer Santini's deputy Jol the job, and he seized his chance. He built an entertaining side that established itself in the top third of the table, and importantly took Spurs back into European competition. But the suspicion was always there that the club's board were not entirely comfortable with the fact that Jol was not their first choice. When the 2007 season began inauspiciously, he was dismissed, and replaced by the moment's next great prospect, Juande Ramos, who had made his mark with Sevilla in La Liga.

Ramos took Jol's team to another League Cup victory in 2008 but the new model soon fell apart and the club continued on its round of managerial musical chairs, grasping at the glory – most notably under Harry Redknapp – but never quite holding on. The streetwise, personable Redknapp appeared an unlikely accomplice for Spurs chairman Daniel Levy but the pairing of this football odd couple gave the fans glimpses of the Spurs they craved.

The team played some attractive football and embarked on a glorious maiden run in the Champions League. Some of the old swagger and identity returned. But Redknapp's frequent reminders that Spurs were lucky to be achieving anything grated, with a substantial section of the support viewing him as self-serving. In the cut-throat world of modern football self-preservation may have been advisable, but when someone seems to put themselves before the club it never goes down well.

Redknapp was ousted and replaced by yet another manager of the moment – André Villas-Boas. Unsurprisingly it didn't work out, and once again a volte-face was executed, and it was back to drawing on internal resources and a more traditional British approach under Tim Sherwood. The club, though, was riven with factions as the managerial chair spun again. The draw and power of the Spurs Way on the collective psyche was still there, but it needed reviving and rethinking for the modern world.

Enter Mauricio Pochettino and the transformation of Spurs from a Europa League club into a Champions League club.

2

Those Glory Glory Nights

'IT'S MAGNIFICENT to be in Europe, and this club – a club like Tottenham Hotspur – if we're not in Europe… we're nothing. We're nothing.' The words of the great Bill Nicholson continue to resonate even in a football world totally transformed from their era in which his Spurs side ruled the roost. Since its inception in 1955, UEFA's European competitions have always been at the heart of Tottenham Hotspur, the very essence of its being. Spurs, it is often forgotten, together with Manchester United, helped blaze a trail for British clubs in Europe.

Bill Nick was one of a select group of enlightened pioneers who saw that, in order to develop, British teams needed to test themselves against the best Europe had to offer, rather than patronisingly assume a position of superior insularity just because the modern game had been founded and codified in Britain.

In 1955 Chelsea, the English champions, at the request of the Football League, declined the invitation to participate in the inaugural European Cup, with the League Secretary Fred Howarth dismissing the competition as 'something of a joke' and 'at best, a nine-day wonder'. The following year, Manchester United manager Matt Busby, believing that 'challenges should be met and not avoided', defied the League and took his team into the European Cup. United reached the semi-finals and, having retained the title, participated again in 1957. The harrowing nature of the tragic plane crash in Munich on 6 February 1958 that killed eight of the supremely gifted Busby Babes team, along with 15 others, was exacerbated in the public's eyes because the European Cup fired their imagination, and there was a sense that Busby could fulfil his destiny and wrest the trophy from Real Madrid, who had won the first two tournaments.

Real went on to dominate the competition. In 1960 they overpowered Eintracht Frankfurt 7-3 in front of 134,000 spectators at Hampden Park – and millions watching live on Eurovision – to lift their fifth European

Cup in a row, now firmly established as Europe's paramount competition, the pinnacle of club football. That Glasgow extravaganza is still described as one of the greatest football matches ever played on these shores.

This then, was the context in which Bill Nick's Double-winning Super Spurs entered the competition in 1961, the enticing prospect of England's 'team of the century' taking on Europe's best.

If Spurs began with any complacency, they were immediately brought down to earth with a 4-2 loss in the heart of the Silesian coalfields to Polish champions Gornik Zabrze. But the return leg at White Hart Lane set the template for this and all future European excursions. Playing in all white under floodlights, Spurs swept their opponents aside to run out 8-1 winners. A crowd of nearly 57,000 roared them on, including three who paraded the touchline dressed as angels in retort to the reprimand by the Polish media who had described Spurs as 'no angels'. The crowd picked up on the angels' good-natured response, the chant *Glory Glory Tottenham Hotspur* was born and grew into the anthem which has accompanied the team down the years.

Spurs went on to reach the semi-finals, narrowly losing out over two legs to the holders, Béla Guttmann's great Benfica side that went on to retain the title after defeating Real Madrid 5-3 in the final. The second leg, a 2-1 pyrrhic victory – the Portuguese went through 4-3 on aggregate after a shot from Mackay scraped the bar as the clock ran down and Jimmy Greaves controversially had what looked a legitimate goal ruled out for offside – at White Hart Lane sticks in the memory. A sense of what might have been and what was to come instantly made Europe an essential part of the club's DNA.

The event resonated down the years because of the game in itself, not because of the cash the club banked, or because – to use one of modern football's more irritating phrases – it represented 'getting to the next level'. It was a superb game of football period, played by two of the best teams in Europe – entertaining, absorbing, glorious. It was a spectacle in and of itself, and all the better for it.

These days it is easy to see the Champions League as a basic prerequisite for any ambitious team, and regretfully the magic and mystery of those early years has been replaced in some cases by a false sense of entitlement. But qualifying for Europe in the 60s was a truly special feeling. And at Spurs that feeling of wonder has never really gone away. Critics may scoff and say that is because absence makes the heart grow fonder, but by not taking European football for granted the romance for all at the club has been sustained and a new glorious chapter eventually ushered in.

Spurs retained the FA Cup in 1962, beating Burnley 3-1 in the final, and thus qualified for the now-defunct European Cup Winners' Cup. The success of the European Cup prompted UEFA to introduce a second competition, one for national cup winners, in 1961. Glasgow Rangers, in a much-hyped 'Battle of Britain', were overcome along with Slovan Bratislava and OFK Belgrade to reach the final in Rotterdam to face highly fancied Atlético Madrid.

In what was described as one of the largest movements of people in Europe outside wartime, thousands of fans crossed the Channel to support their team. They were handsomely rewarded when Spurs turned in what, years later, two-goal hero Terry Dyson said was 'probably our best team performance' and such was the resultant elation after an assured, unequivocal 5-1 thrashing that even the normally reticent Bill Nick joined in the celebrations. 'It was about the only time Bill ever came out with the team,' recalled Dyson in the official club history *The Glory Glory Nights*. 'I don't think that I ever saw him looking so pleased.'

The supporters followed their side's pioneering example, organising themselves to travel to destinations across Europe to watch their team at a time when intercontinental travel was exotic. From the start of the club's European adventures, they chartered planes and arranged trips, largely through a company called Riviera Holidays. The club thought arranging travel too risky a business. Based in London's Bishopsgate, Riviera was run by enterprising Spurs fan Aubrey Morris, a former London cabbie who went on to develop the concept of the package holiday. A pioneer indeed.

At only his second attempt, Bill Nick had achieved his ambition of showing that his team was as good as any, and better than most, in Europe. He made history as the first British manager to triumph in Europe, a chart topper that can never be bettered. Motivated by the feeling that, despite prevailing in the FA Cup Final, they had failed to do themselves justice on a showcase occasion, Spurs felt they had to put down a marker for the history books. They accomplished it in spades and in typical flamboyant style.

A tradition had been established, a solid foundation laid. Under Bill Nick's guidance Spurs had become a permanent fixture in the top half of the top division (also FA Cup winners in 1967), always threatening to take a seat at Europe's top table again but never quite managing it. With players such as Pat Jennings, Steve Perryman, Alan Mullery, Martin Chivers and the sublimely talented Alan Gilzean, the original King of White Hart Lane, Spurs were well prepared for an assault on the inaugural UEFA Cup, introduced in 1972 for clubs a few steps away from league glory. They began in definitive fashion, smashing 15 goals over two legs past Icelandic side Keflavik, then scraped through against Nantes before rediscovering their poise against the Romanians Rapid Bucharest and UT Arad.

For fans of an impressionable age, these European ventures opened up new vistas. When drawn against a totally unfamiliar opponent such as UT Arad, maps and atlases would be eagerly consulted to find out where and in what country the teams came from. It all added to the feeling that Spurs and their fans were privileged, were something special.

Something special was what the club had promised the players, their wives and families if they reached the final, a trip to whatever city their opponents were from. Most were less than amused when the opponents turned out to be Wolverhampton Wanderers. They would naturally have preferred Milan who were edged out in two tight semi-final tussles, courtesy of three goals from two unlikely scorers, a brace (his second a fulminating strike from 35 yards) from Steve Perryman and Alan Mullery who, ostracised for much of the season by Bill Nick, had been brought back from a loan spell with Fulham.

With the atmosphere more akin to a league game than a European final, Spurs overcame Wolves 3-2 over two legs to become the first British side to win two European competitions. The 2-1 win at Molineux was down to Martin Chivers. According to Hunter Davies in his seminal book *The Glory Game*: 'He'd simply risen to the occasion, turning on two moments of deadly accuracy, while all around him lesser players had been rushing, bustling and getting nowhere.' Chivers' second, a long-range strike that rose inexorably into the back of the net, is still remembered as one of the great European goals.

The final provided a fitting stage for captain Alan Mullery to say farewell – another rare goal of his secured the home 1-1 draw – after nine seasons. At the final whistle he was carried around the field in triumph deserted by his team-mates who had run to the safety of the dressing room as the fans invaded the pitch. The joyous feeling of winning a European trophy on your own ground in a home tie is one that will never be experienced again now that finals are played at neutral venues. Lucky Spurs fans would experience it twice in a decade. It's part of what made White Hart Lane such a special ground.

The following season, Spurs held on to their trophy until the semi-final before succumbing on away goals to the eventual winners, Bill Shankly's Liverpool. In 1974 they went one better and reached the final against Feyenoord before losing ignominiously amid rioting in Rotterdam. In vain, Bill Nick made repeated appeals to stop the violence and the shocking scenes he witnessed that night almost certainly influenced his decision to walk away from the game he loved. Many true Spurs fans shared the manager's embarrassment and, shamed by the hooligan element, seriously considered their commitment.

As a result of the mayhem, Spurs were banned from Europe but the ban was never implemented as the team went into decline and failed to qualify. For seven years they drifted, even losing their place in the first division. It was left to a new incarnation of Spurs under a new, young manager, Keith Burkinshaw, to restore their fortunes, firstly by taking them back to the First Division and then providing, once again, a succession of glory nights on the European stage.

On 14 May 1981, Tottenham Hotspur had a glory glory night with a difference – not against a foreign opponent under the lights at White Hart Lane, but a replay of the Centenary FA Cup Final at Wembley against Manchester City. Ricky Villa scored one of the greatest goals seen in a Wembley final to enable Spurs to lift the FA Cup for the sixth time and take them back to the promised land once again. (They had a lot to live up to as in their absence England, courtesy of Liverpool and Nottingham Forest, monopolised the European Cup, with the winning sequence extended to six in a row by Aston Villa in 1982.)

Spurs' return to Dutch soil in 1981 provided some sense of squaring a circle. The opposition was Ajax, and the tie was as good as wrapped up by a 3-1 victory. Moreover, the travelling support's good behaviour went some way towards restoring besmirched reputations. Dundalk and Eintracht Frankfurt were dispatched before the semi-final against Barcelona. Many sides had come to White Hart Lane with the intention of nullifying Spurs' attacking prowess but none had employed such cynical, spiteful tactics; a shameful antithesis to the attractive, record-breaking contemporary Barcelona sides. It was an ugly night which ended in a 1-1 stalemate. In Spain the season's exertions – four league games were played in the fortnight between the two legs – caught up with Spurs and despite a valiant performance they lost by a solitary goal. (Complaints that the English authorities do little to help their clubs in Europe are nothing new.) Tony Galvin recalled that Brian Glanville, the doyen of English football writers, had told him 'it was a set-up because the final was going to be in Barcelona'. And Paul Miller lamented: 'We were the best team in Europe that year. Barcelona kicked us out.' Keith Burkinshaw, though, took a positive view of events. 'If this is failure,' he declared, 'I want more of it'. His wish would be duly granted.

Having competed manfully for four trophies, at the end of a gruelling season Spurs were left with just one, the FA Cup. This took them back into Europe but the stay proved to be short-lived, the journey ending in the second round in the fog of Munich's Olympic Stadium against an accomplished Bayern. However, another fourth-placed finish in the league saw a return to Europe for a third time in a row, this time in the UEFA Cup once more.

Reminding Bill Nick, back on the staff in an advisory role, of the good old days, the 1983/84 campaign turned out to be a classic Spurs story. It began with a 14-0 drubbing of Drogheda United from the Republic of Ireland. The momentum continued with the visit of old foes Feyenoord, led by Johan Cruyff in the twilight of his playing career. The maestro was keen to test himself against a star pupil who proceeded to overshadow him with a sublime display. 'Hoddle was a player I liked,' revealed Cruyff in a gracious accolade, 'but it was only on the pitch I realised just how good he really was. He played football the way I wanted to see it played.' Spurs skipper Steve Perryman summed up the 4-2 win as 'probably the best Spurs performance I'd ever been involved in' (and there were 854 of them).

Poor league form was put to one side as Spurs went marching on. Revenge was gained against Bayern Munich, then came FK Austria and, on a tumultuous night in front of over 40,000 at White Hart Lane, Hajduk Split were edged out on away goals. Just days before the tie was played, Burkinshaw had announced he would be leaving at the end of the season. The final against Anderlecht was to be his swansong. And victory was also the only way he could leave the club with a ticket to Europe for the following season.

The first leg in Belgium ended 1-1, but reserve goalkeeper Tony Parks, who took the place of the injured Ray Clemence, recalling the tie years later, said the players were confident they'd set things up well enough to win at home. 'European nights at White Hart Lane were brilliant,' he said. 'When that Shelf side was packed out it was awesome.' If truth be told the match itself was certainly nothing special, but what unfolded was one of the classic European nights in N17, undeniable drama that only sport is capable of delivering.

With over 46,000 watching inside the stadium and millions more on television, the denouement came down to a penalty shootout after a last-gasp equaliser from Graham Roberts had kept Spurs alive and two exhausted sides played out an inconclusive 30 minutes of extra time. The tension was almost unbearable. Parks gave Spurs the advantage by saving Anderlecht's first kick, but young defender Danny Thomas missed what could have been the winning penalty. Thomas was distraught. The crowd, in a spontaneous response seared into the consciousness of every fan who witnessed it, boomed out 'There's only one Danny Thomas'. Everything came down to the last kick. Arnór Guðjohnsen stepped up, struck the ball… and Parks went the right way and saved it. As the stadium erupted, the goalkeeper memorably ran full pelt down the pitch before finally being caught and mobbed by jubilant team-mates. Although Parks made fewer than 50 appearances for the club, the glory glory night he gave the fans was rewarded with them granting him legendary status.

On the cusp of disintegrating, this Spurs team had its reward. A very good manager had his fond farewell. And his team had secured a European trophy at its own home for the second time.

The next UEFA Cup campaign was something of an anti-climax as the holders unluckily went out in the fourth round by a single goal to Real Madrid. It was a sad end to a fourth successive campaign for the 1980s side. Paul Miller succinctly summed up its legacy: 'Europe was made for us. That team was suited to Europe, more possibly than to the English league.'

A long fallow period followed, with Spurs not returning to Europe until 1991/92 for a brief crack at the Cup Winners' Cup, and again in 1999/2000, this time in the UEFA Cup. The teams were pale shadows of the cup-winning sides of the 1960s, 70s and 80s. It wasn't until Martin Jol took the Lilywhites back into Europe in 2006/07 in the UEFA Cup that the old Euro magic got the fans in its spell again. Even then, the glory was tempered by the circumstances of qualification. Finishing in the top four would have sent Spurs into the Champions League, the old-style knockout cup having been replaced in 1992 to provide more guaranteed games and more money for the participants. But on the last day of the season at West Ham's Upton Park, a Spurs side ravaged by a virus were heartbreakingly beaten, thereby conceding the coveted fourth spot to Arsenal of all teams.

Nonetheless, as the 2006/07 campaign began, the stadium buzzed again in anticipation as the sight of the all-white kits under the floodlights and opponents from the Continent connected the present, an ambitious Premier League club, to the glories of the past. The competition was now in a group format and four home wins were recorded in front of packed houses before Spurs stumbled at the quarter-final stage. However, a second successive fifth-place finish in the league enabled them to have another go the following season. But Spurs appeared to be on the slide. An unedifying night at White Hart Lane saw Getafe beat Spurs as rumours, that unfortunately turned out to be all too true, that Jol had been sacked swirled around the stands. New boss Juande Ramos could only take Spurs to round four and, despite steering the club back into Europe, only lasted till round three of the 2008/09 UEFA Cup.

It would take until 2010/11 for Spurs to assume their seat at the top table for the first time since 1962, edging out Manchester City in the penultimate league game in what was effectively a play-off for the last Champions League place. A goal by Peter Crouch eight minutes from time enabled them to scrape through. In retrospect it turned out to be the richest game in Spurs' history.

European football had changed dramatically. The Champions League was now the only game in town. To underline the point, at the end of the campaign Spurs had banked €31.1m from UEFA (participation bonus, match bonus, performance bonus and share of TV pool) while vanquished Manchester City, who admittedly reached one round fewer in the Europa Cup, only took home €6.1m.

Against all predictions, Harry Redknapp's Spurs lit up the group stage, heading the group and along the way becoming the first Champions League club to score two or more goals in all six of their group games. The highlights were two extraordinary games against reigning champions Inter Milan. In Italy, with some 6,000 travelling supporters watching from the away section, Spurs appeared to be down and out when, at half-time, Inter were four goals to the good. But in a never-to-be-forgotten second half, and with Spurs down to ten men, Gareth Bale announced himself as a world class talent with a hat-trick that stunned the hosts. 'There was space to turn into so I just made the most of it,' Bale modestly explained, 'and as soon as I had a sight of goal I had a go. Thankfully it worked.' And how.

As the clock ticked down, the home fans were frantically whistling for the referee to blow for time as their side reeled from wave after wave of attacks. And this was just an appetiser – there was more to come in the return game. Bale turned in another masterclass, Spurs were sublime, and with the fans in raptures the old stadium shook with delight. The atmosphere was electrifying. As Bale once again sailed past Inter's Brazilian international full-back, then rated one of the best in the world, a roar emerged from the depths of the stands and carried and rolled around and around the ground. 'Taxi for Maicon, taxi for Maicon.' Spurs fans were in dreamland. That old European magic was back. The 3-1 win was summed up by Henry Winter in *The Daily Telegraph* as 'the sort of scintillating performance to intoxicate younger minds among the Lane faithful and remind older heads of the glory glory nights'.

Redknapp's men returned to Milan after qualifying, against all predictions. What's more, they topped their group. Their attacking displays had made Europe sit up and take notice, but conversely it was disciplined defensive duties that took them past AC Milan, courtesy of a single Peter Crouch goal, and into a quarter-final against Real Madrid. From the sublime to the foolish; the hero of Milan became the villain of Madrid. Already a goal down, a red card for the centre-forward effectively ended the glory glory trail as Real put four past Heurelho Gomes and one more for good measure in the return leg.

The following year it was back to the bread and butter of the Europa League and nothing seemed the same. A taste of glory gone all too soon. The glory and, probably above all, the money to be gained from the Champions League – it was a benevolent double whammy as the minimum requirement was fourth place in the Premier League which in itself was worth £100m – encouraged Spurs to regard the Europa League as very much the poor relation, the booby prize. So with eyes firmly fixed on the Premier League, Harry Redknapp and his successors André Villas-Boas, Tim Sherwood and Mauricio Pochettino rang the changes – otherwise euphemistically termed a rotation policy – to often put out less than the best available eleven to represent the club, with the concomitant poor results. In five consecutive Europa League seasons between 2011 and 2016 a solitary quarter-final was recorded. For supporters, European nights were becoming a chore – it was Spurs in Europe, but not really Spurs in Europe. Poor performances, disjointed teams, a sense of not wanting to be present pervading both pitch and stands. A strange kind of glory.

Then in 2016, glory be, Mauricio Pochettino's Spurs made it back into the Champions League. Poch regarded Champions League football with much the same fervour as Bill Nick had valued competing in Europe. But this was a different era, and while Poch's approach connected with all the Spurs Way represented, it was very much the personable Argentinian's own interpretation. Three successive appearances in the Champions League demonstrated that after all the years of mediocrity and disappointment and the fleeting glimmer of glory, Spurs and their supporters could actually reach for the stars and not be castigated for it.

3

He's magic, you know

SERENADED BY fans with an adaptation of Scottish pop band Pilot's 1974 hit *Magic*, Poch has, in his five years at the club, created a team very much in his own image, yet one that is recognisably consistent with the Spurs Way.

The achievement has been accomplished by efforts more material than magic, but Poch himself is not averse to drawing on a little mysticism to explain his beliefs. Of course, he uses data, in fact reams of it, but controlling the positive/negative energy sources is, in his mind, the key factor in decision making. Hence the lemons on his desk at the training ground to attract the negative energy that he believes some people arrive with. It is a measure of the respect he has earned that in the macho world he works in, such eccentric ideas have not been treated with eye-rolling scorn.

When he came to Spurs, Poch says, it was clear that there was no magic formula to deal with the situation he found. His appointment was not universally popular, with some fans questioning whether he was a big enough name. Even so chairman Daniel Levy explained: 'I wanted someone who believes in the way I think we ought to operate, so that's why I went for Mauricio.' Specifically, his preference for developing talent rather than hiring top of the bill stars for a quick fix. Poch's loyalty to his previous employers, Southampton, his erstwhile boss Nicola Cortese and players was a point in his favour. Too often in the seasons preceding his arrival, Spurs had the feel of a soap opera, with various characters and factions conducting their business and voicing their disagreements in public. The consequent media circus was anathema to Levy, who does not relish the limelight, so Poch's understated approach, his avoidance of grandstanding, appealed. Poch's preference, while at Southampton, for conducting interviews in his native Spanish certainly helped avoid, through any misunderstanding of the nuances of a foreign language, getting drawn into media mind games.

Perhaps he saw the ruse as preserving some mystique. However, at Spurs, it was made clear from the outset that the manager was expected to communicate directly in English with the players, the media and the fans. Poch's linguistic ability was soon being deftly deployed.

During his tenure at the club the Chairman has frequently been criticised by fans for not investing enough in the playing side. Whether a certain player could or should have been signed at any particular time will always, to a large extent, be a matter of subjective judgement and Spurs simply did not have the financial wherewithal to compete with the European powerhouses. Spurs may be owned by one of the world's richest men, multi-billionaire tax exile Joe Lewis, but this owner was no Roman Abramovich or Sheikh Mansour, willing to inject vast sums to buy a route to the top. So, from the start, his hands-on younger, junior partner sought to prioritise the youth academy and training facilities.

There was one notable departure from that approach when, in the summer of 2013 and with André Villas-Boas in charge, after selling Gareth Bale to Real Madrid for a then world record fee of £86m, Spurs spent £106.5m on seven players. In came Roberto Soldado,

Érik Lamela, Étienne Capoue, Vlad Chiriches, Paulinho, Nacer Chadli and Christian Eriksen. Only Eriksen has been an unqualified success, and only he and Lamela – whose star has flickered but never consistently shone – remain at the club. Proof, as Levy likes to point out, that splashing the cash does not guarantee success. Not if you buy the wrong players. Moreover, there was the impression that the lack of acumen in the transfer market was also illustrated by missed opportunities. At vital moments, managers – Poch was the eighth since 2001 – had not been fully supported, allowing key signings that could have taken the team forward to slip away.

There are numerous examples of Spurs spending lavishly to great effect, from Bill Nick's great teams to the current squad. Spurs historically have bought superstars. Heroes all from Danny Blanchflower to Jürgen Klinsmann, remembered with as much affection as those rare jewels – such as Steve Perryman, Glenn Hoddle and Ledley King – who emerged from the youth academy. The Spurs Way was built and maintained by many high-profile, big-money signings, and the expectation that the club will demonstrate its clout and its ambition by spending big is lodged deep within the supporter psyche.

Of necessity, the business model of developing players took on greater significance. And the more the Chairman talked up the new training centre, the potential new stadium and the rosy long-term future, the more necessary it became to demonstrate progress. And there has been progress, but not quite in the way it was envisaged. Admittedly Spurs have developed talent, but often it was originally unearthed elsewhere – most notably Dele Alli who, supporters delight in reminding all and sundry, 'only cost five mil'. Under Poch's guidance graduates may have flourished at the training complex in Enfield, but in many cases they were not planted there. Notable exceptions can be counted on the fingers of one hand. Harry Kane was a product of the club's youth academy, Ryan Mason another, a Spurs fan who grew up with the club and who subsequently formed a key component of Poch's first team. Harry Winks, a Spurs man born and bred, who stands on the brink of establishing himself as a first-team and England international mainstay, is justifiably lauded as 'one of our own'. But the harsh reality is that the trio are the only ones who have survived the tough trip from the academy to the first team in Poch's five years at the club.

The manager is surely frustrated with the meagre return as he gives the impression that he would rather promote from within than use the cheque book. Unless Poch is certain that an expensive transfer can bring him something extra, he feels that his team would probably be better off without that player; a salutary lesson he probably learned from acquiring Vincent Janssen, yet another expensive striking sensation from the Netherlands who failed to deliver in the Premier League (though there have been notable exceptions, namely Ruud van Nistelrooy and Luis Suárez). His preference would be youngsters who dreamed of playing for the club and have a sense of identity. If they are made of the right stuff, they won't forget who nurtured them and gave them a chance and will thus be more likely to show full commitment and loyalty. Poch tries to get them to believe in him as a way of believing in themselves.

The other success stories on the playing staff have certainly benefitted from the manager's coaching and motivational skills, but all had begun to build a reputation outside North London. Son Heung-min was arguably already a star when he joined from Bayer Leverkusen in 2015 for the not inconsiderable sum of £22m. Hugo Lloris, a French international, had earned a nomination as UEFA Goalkeeper of the Year when he arrived from Lyon in 2012; Mousa Dembélé came from Fulham; Kyle Walker from Sheffield United; Danny Rose from Leeds; and Eric Dier from Sporting Lisbon. Jan Vertonghen, Toby Alderweireld and Davinson Sánchez were products of the Ajax youth academy, as was Eriksen.

What all Poch's men have in common is that however they arrived at his door, they all come with or soon learn to adopt the right attitude, namely that they love the game, regard it as a privilege and a passion, a pleasurable end in itself and not an easy route to fame and fortune. Like all top contemporary sports people a commitment to a positive lifestyle is mandatory; the English bingeing culture (the wrong food and alcohol excess) consigned to the waste bin of yesteryear, players are expected to take good care of themselves with the right diet, rest and exercise. Importantly, training should never be viewed as a chore but a necessary process along the way to fulfilment as individuals, players and a team. And certainly not as a way of sweating out the alcohol from the night before. The sense of team spirit is important and probably explains why Poch has often chosen to keep the novices he really rates close by rather than send them out on loan. If they are to be taught in the right way, best that it is undertaken at home where he can keep a paternal eye on them.

Handsomely rewarded for what they are paid to do, the time and effort spent on providing the best for them on and off the pitch is expected to be appreciated. And in return, Poch doesn't demand that they win at all costs, just that they always endeavour to give full commitment to the cause.

Like many successful South American coaches, Poch was inspired by Marcelo Bielsa for whom he played at Newell's Old Boys and, for a short period, at Espanyol before Bielsa left to coach the national team. Poch was promptly called up for his international debut and went on to play another 19 times for Argentina at centre-back. Not so obsessed with the opposition as 'El Loco' – who is? – Poch sets his teams out in a fluid 4-3-3 formation – 4-3-3, 4-2-3-1, 4-5-1, facilitating changes during the course of 90 minutes according to the dictates of the game. Controlled possession, starting at the back and with an intensive mindset to impose a high tempo and press to discomfort the opposition. He demands that they are always proactive to compete intensely, a style he feels is eminently suited to the Premier League.

Leaving Southampton, a team that was desperately keen to avoid relegation from the Premier League (which they achieved), when Poch arrived at Spurs in the 2014 pre-season he found to his dismay a squad that appeared to be aimless and drifting. With the Chairman's backing he embarked on a remarkable journey. Some players didn't want to accompany him, others fell by the wayside but crucially he had the necessary time to effect the transformation he desired, commencing with tighter training procedures and stricter disciplinary measures.

Essential to the process were Poch's three assistants – Jesús Perez, Toni Jiménez and Miguel D'Agostino – who together with him as their leader comprise the four *amigos*. 'A group effort', according to Poch, as revealed to Guillem Balague in *Brave New World,* an intimate portrait of Poch and his Spurs across the 2016/17 season, … 'a coaching team who believe in a way of playing and a way of living… but I have the final word'. He also has the final word on transfers, as long as they are within budget, though not on contracts and salaries which are the province of the Chairman.

Jesús Perez is the *de facto* number two who assists his boss with coaching and is the conduit through which the back-up specialists operate. Miguel D'Agostino is in charge of scouting and Toni Jiménez, who played with Poch at Espanyol, the goalkeeping coach. Unlike most of his ilk more importance is attached to Jiménez's role as many moves in a Poch team – as is the case with Pep Guardiola's Manchester City, who have set the gold standard – start with the goalkeeper, whether it is a gradual build-up from the back or an instant long ball forward.

Poch respects and admires Sir Alex Ferguson. But while Fergie constantly refreshed his back-room staff and distanced himself from coaching, Poch feels that, together with his three *compadres*, this is a coaching group keen to learn and improve and challenge each other, so there is no need for outside help. He is in his element on the training field. In fact, the cabal is so insular that although Ossie Ardiles, Poch's close friend and hero when he was growing up, is a regular visitor to his office, intimate team and player discussions are off limits in their chats together.

Eleven games into the 2014/15 Premier League season and alarm bells sounded. Spurs slumped to a home defeat against Stoke City that was so inept they were booed off by their own fans. The line-up was a mix of established names and the younger players who had been given their chance by Poch's predecessor Tim Sherwood. It was reported that the newcomers, led by Kane and Mason, confronted the older clan in the dressing room and questioned their attitude. The heated exchange showed Poch who was made of the right stuff and who his disciples would be. Jan Vertonghen later told *The Daily Mirror* that there were 'no longer any heroes' in the Spurs team. 'When one makes a mistake, the other one picks it up. We have a togetherness.'

Forging that team spirit was the key. There was now a clear direction and on New Year's Day 2015 Spurs showed what they could do with a blistering display that saw Chelsea ripped apart and sent home nursing a 5-3 drubbing. The Blues fans' bragging about 'Three Point Lane' had been comprehensively silenced. Poch had observed on his arrival that Spurs had historically been synonymous with a certain style of football. London clubs, exemplified by Spurs, were regarded by their Northern counterparts as 'All fur coat and no knickers', flash geezers with no substance. Were Spurs ready to show their critics that their game was about both glory and winning?

Poch's second full season in charge seemed to deliver the answer. Against all expectations, Spurs were in contention for the Premier League title until the final days of the season. Manchester United, Manchester City, Chelsea, Arsenal and Liverpool were pushed aside as upstarts, Spurs and Leicester City led the pack, but it was against London rivals Chelsea that the dreams of a first title since 1961 were dashed. On the evening of 2 May 2016, Spurs travelled to Stamford Bridge, a ground where they had not won for 26 years. A draw in the previous game against West Bromwich Albion had effectively put paid to any realistic title aspirations, and it was now down to the final roll of the dice. Spurs had to win to stay in the hunt.

By half-time they were 2-0 up. So far, so good. The frenetic atmosphere had been stoked by some robust challenges and in the second half the game boiled over. Spurs' players lost their heads, picking up a record nine yellow cards. Chelsea pulled a goal back and then, seven minutes from time, Eden Hazard levelled, and Tottenham's title dreams were truly over and done with.

What became known as the Battle of the Bridge was one of the most high-octane matches in the history of a high-octane derby, but while Spurs fans went away deflated and dispirited, there was slight consolation to be had that their reputation for being a soft touch had been well and truly shaken off. Spurs had certainly shown they would not be intimidated, but while they appeared to have shown their mettle, the truth was they could still be knocked off their game. They not only lost their heads, but the two-goal lead they desperately needed. In mitigation, it could be argued that they succumbed to some serious provocation from their opponents compounded by a bizarre refereeing performance by Mark Clattenburg whose post-match comments that he 'allowed Spurs to self-destruct' certainly raised a few questions on the way he had carried out his duties (Clattenburg would go on to defend his actions, saying that if he'd sent players off he would have been accused of costing Spurs the title). All the same, Spurs combusted and in those circumstances the role of the manager is firmly in the spotlight. Could Poch have done more at half-time to calm his players? When composure was needed, Spurs had been found lacking. It was unlikely that he told them 'we have been lucky. We have got away with it. Chelsea have lost their heads. If we keep cool we will win.' If he did it certainly fell on deaf ears.

The season tailed off in anti-climax at St James' Park as Spurs were thrashed 5-1 by the already-relegated Newcastle United. Many more Spurs fans than the official allocation of 3,000 had travelled in anticipation that they would have something to celebrate. In the final analysis, with the winning post in sight the team failed to adhere to the principles that had served them so well and taken them so far.

Poch took the defeat personally. Was it his fault they had played so poorly? He asked himself again and again. Relinquishing the runners-up spot to Arsenal, of all teams – prompting the jibe that Spurs had contrived to finish third in a two-horse race – was costly both emotionally and in the pocket. Dropping a league place was not only an exorbitant loss in itself but reduced the percentage share from the forthcoming Champions League television pool. So the Newcastle fiasco alone turned out to be a financial hit of at least £6 million. Perhaps just as worrying was the doubt it lodged in the manager's mind. Was it indicative of a fundamental flaw he hadn't envisaged, one that needed to be identified and rectified if the team were to progress? While the drama at Stamford Bridge positioned the encounter in the popular narrative as the pivotal moment, the game against West Brom arguably inflicted more significant damage. Spurs had been a goal up, but let the lead slip in a performance that exuded weariness and a lack of ambition. For all the cutting comments about Spurs being 'bottlers', the fact remained that they had been the only team to chase Leicester down to the wire, and that the Foxes who had kept on piling up the points had won the title rather than being the beneficiaries of Spurs letting it slip. The delight with which fans in other parts of the capital revelled at Spurs' discomfort gave some indication that they were now seen as a genuine threat. And when the dust settled there was the consolation that they were back dining at the top European table.

Change was in the air and as plans for Spurs' impressive, eye-popping new stadium were finally put into practice, White Hart Lane saw its capacity cut as the north-east corner was demolished to make way for the future. The ground now held just 31,500 people, further reducing matchday revenue that was already the lowest of the top Premier League clubs. Moreover, once the stringent requirements insisted upon by UEFA for their competitions were assessed, it was apparent that White Hart Lane would not be able to accommodate all season-ticket holders, all corporate and executive guests, and all the media. These obligations, together with the anticipated fall in matchday revenues, forced the club to look again at Wembley to host its Champions League games.

The request was granted, but while the decision enabled many more fans to see their team, and prepared them for the season Spurs would have to spend away from N17 during the rebuild, it meant that the proud tradition of European football at White Hart Lane had slipped away unheralded. The final game had been a prosaic 2-1 round of 16 Europa League loss to Borussia Dortmund. It was left to the impressive and colourful away support to bring down the curtain on an historic European venue.

The move to Wembley ushered in a new era. Feelings were stirred at the prospect of welcoming the 2016/17 Champions League to the national stadium, and an inspired decision to discount prices for fans prepared to subscribe for all three home group games, before the opponents or match dates were confirmed, helped ensure that 85,011 were present for the visit of Monaco in September. It was Spurs' highest ever home attendance, the largest home attendance recorded by an English league club in any competition, and the highest ever home attendance for an English club in the Champions League. To complement the historic playing kit, the club asked fans to try and wear white for the night, and the sight of Wembley Way transformed into a sea of white was one to behold and cherish.

Unfortunately, in an example of what was now termed as being 'Spursy' by critics, they fluffed their lines, losing 2-1 in a lacklustre showing. Poch reflected that his team lacked passion – a rare instance of public criticism. The debacle at Newcastle at the end of the previous season still weighed on his mind. He questioned himself and his men. What was wrong with the mentality?

Spurs travelled to Moscow for matchday two and ran out 1-0 winners with an unspectacular but assured display against CSKA. A further point from a 0-0 draw in Germany against Bayer Leverkusen left Spurs second in a group where the four teams were separated by just three points. Beating Bayer at Wembley would see Spurs through, but in front of another record-breaking crowd of 85,512 they lost 1-0 after a display Poch labelled 'embarrassing'.

Needing victory in Monaco to reach the knockout stage, Spurs went a goal down early in the second half, equalised through a penalty, then conceded within four kicks of the restart. They were unceremoniously dumped out of the Champions League having only scored one goal from open play. Once again Poch took an important reverse personally. He blamed himself for failing to communicate with the players just how important the competition was. Their failure to do themselves justice was not, he felt, down to any lack of quality but the inability to change their approach at a few days' notice for the different tasks that awaited them. He determined that, should the opportunity come again, he would be ready, willing and able.

Meanwhile, as December arrived Spurs had to face the ignominy of scrapping for a Europa League place reserved for the third-placed Champions League group finishers. It was a competition they hoped they had left behind for good, and one which Poch – like several of his predecessors – clearly didn't see as a priority. But a win was needed for pride and to put talk of a Wembley wobble to bed. Only 62,034 turned up for the game against CSKA Moscow – although that was still more than could be accommodated in the new ground the club was building – to see Spurs run out convincing 3-1 victors.

Drawn away against Belgian side Gent in the first knockout round in the Europa League, Spurs turned in yet another disjointed and lacklustre display. Europe, where Spurs so longed to be, was becoming a Thursday night ordeal, and the performances were far below those in the Premier League that had brought victories over Chelsea and Manchester City and kept the team very much involved in a second successive title race. Some 80,465 turned up for the second leg hoping to see a 1-0 deficit overturned, a record for a Europa League tie, realised in large part because entry prices had been slashed – there was a plethora of £5 tickets – together with a large contingent of Belgian fans.

Sad to say, Spurs could only draw 2-2, and tumbled out of the competition on a night that also saw Dele Alli sent off for a shocking high tackle that would see him banned if Spurs returned to Europe.

This latest European adventure had been a largely unfulfilling experience, only the vast crowds at Wembley and UEFA's largesse providing any kind of compensation. In contrast, the home front continued to sparkle. Between 14 December and the end of the season on 21 May, Spurs lost only twice in the league. Unfortunately, the second defeat continued a newly acquired habit of forfeiting their title opportunity at the home of a London rival, the 0-1 scoreline at West Ham ensuring that a Chelsea team untroubled by the need to compete in Europe were crowned as champions.

Spurs put the downer behind them by overcoming Manchester United 2-1, maintaining an undefeated home record, on an emotional afternoon at the last game at White Hart Lane before the bulldozers moved in. The season ended on a high note as Leicester City and Hull City were walloped 6-1 and 7-1 respectively, Kane scoring seven goals and securing the Golden Boot in the process. Spurs finished second, on 86 points, five more than Leicester attained when they were crowned champions the year before.

The Newcastle debacle and the miserable Champions League campaign had finally been laid to rest, together with the notion that Spurs always fudged the business end of the season, their abject loss to their nemesis Chelsea in the FA Cup semi-final notwithstanding. Lessons had been learned and it was with eager anticipation that the Spurs contingent attended the Champions League draw in Monaco.

When it was made they were handed a tough assignment with Real Madrid and Borussia Dortmund. APOEL from Cyprus made up the group. Dortmund were the first opponents, coming to a Wembley now occupied by Spurs for all home games. And already there had been problems. Three league games had been and gone without any sign of a win. Taken together with the dire previous European campaign it looked as if the Wembley wobble had morphed into a full-blown curse. Combined with the fact the group stage ticket package price had been hiked by almost 50% on the previous year, the result was that on the night 'just' 67,343 turned up. But what a night they had as Spurs emphatically put all talk of a Wembley phobia to bed. Son scored after four minutes. Dortmund equalised soon after only for Harry Kane to put the home team ahead again four minutes later. Another from the talismanic striker on the hour secured a 3-1 victory.

The thrilling nature of a pulsating encounter initially obscured the indubitable steps forward Spurs had taken. This was not only another glory glory night, but one in which Spurs had boxed clever. Dortmund had the majority of the possession, but Spurs opted to defend a little deeper than Poch's high press normally demanded, playing on the break to devastating effect. It was Kane's night as the striker created the first and scored two more, his determination, physical strength and eye for both a pass and a goal driving his team-mates on. Jason Burt in *The Daily Telegraph* observed that 'Kane is getting better and better and is beginning to belong in that rarefied company of elite strikers, imposing himself for club and country'. Wembley rose to applaud lustily as he departed the pitch after being substituted late on.

Spurs had sent a message of confidence and trust that they could succeed at their temporary home. Sometimes a season can turn on one game. Had Spurs just played it?

Three more goals, with no reply, against APOEL in Cyprus put Spurs in the best possible position for their trip to the Bernabéu. Once again, Kane shone, and it was his pressure that led Real's Raphaël Varane to put the ball into his own net on 28 minutes. Cristiano Ronaldo levelled from the spot just before half-time, but Spurs continued to ask questions of their hosts, gathering plaudits for a mature performance that tested a team that had won 21 of their previous 23 home Champions League games. Kane, linked by the media in the run-up to the game with the possibility of a big-money move to Real, almost snatched a winner 20 minutes from time, goalkeeper Keylor Navas needing every ounce of his ability to keep his shot out.

The previous year's despondency seemed a long time ago, Spurs were clicking and Poch was showing – in response to grumbles on the fringes that he lacked a plan B – that he was prepared to vary his approach when necessary. The mental strength he had often talked about was there for all to see alongside the entertaining football that had lit up the Premier League for two seasons. Nevertheless, few could have predicted what was to come next.

Quite simply, in the return fixture at Wembley, Spurs played the Champions League holders Real Madrid off the park. 'This was the night when the most successful club side in Europe found out the hard way why Mauricio Pochettino and his players have attracted so much acclaim over the past few years,' wrote *The Guardian*'s Daniel Taylor. On this occasion it was Dele Alli who took centre stage, scoring two, having a vital role in a third and, in an enticing cameo, nutmegging Sergio Ramos for good measure. But this was no one-man show. Kieran Trippier rampaged up and down the right wing, his first-time crosses causing Real no end of problems. Kane was again an impressive figure, and young Harry Winks looked every inch the experienced central midfielder. Spurs' third goal was the pick of the bunch, with Kane and Alli combining to send Christian Eriksen through for a composed finish in a counter-attack of staggering penetrative speed. Nearly 84,000 were inside Wembley that night, and the noise was deafening. Television viewers got an inkling of the atmosphere when the cacophony and celebrations after the great Dane's goal shook the camera transmitting the scenes. It was a glory glory night to rank with the best and, perhaps most pleasingly, *The Guardian*'s Taylor was moved to observe that, when Ronaldo pulled one back with ten minutes to go, it may once have prompted nerves but 'Spurs, frankly, are no longer a side with that kind of soft centre'. Spurs headed a group which contained the 2013 finalists and the holders who had won the competition in three of the past five seasons.

There was mental strength aplenty on display as Spurs made a return to Dortmund for matchday five. They went into the game following a derby defeat to Arsenal, and fell behind to a goal from Aubameyang. With a changed formation that saw Son partner Kane in a front two and Alli and Eriksen dropped deeper to play alongside Winks in the centre of midfield, Spurs fought back to run out 2-1 winners thanks to second-half goals from their front men. For Kane, it was six goals in five Champions League games. For Spurs, the result ensured that they would finish above Real Madrid in the group.

Spurs rounded off the group stage with a 3-0 win over APOEL at Wembley, but any thoughts that topping the group would secure a slightly easier draw in the first knockout stage were dashed as Juventus came out of the hat. At least Spurs had the second leg at home, and travelled to Turin confident they could compete. However, after 74 seconds an all-too-familiar story from yesteryear seemed to be unfolding as defensive chaos allowed Gonzalo Higuaín to volley home a beauty from Miralem Pjanic's smart free kick. Then Ben Davies lunged in on Federico Bernardeschi and Higuaín scored again from the penalty spot. Juventus, who had conceded just one goal in their previous 16 matches, were 2-0 up and coasting. Or so they thought.

This, though was the new, mentally strong Spurs and, from the first quarter onwards they dominated the Italian champions, turning in an exquisite display of passing and attacking football. Chance after chance was created until on 35 minutes, Kane – who else? – rounded Gianluigi Buffon and rolled the ball into the Juve net. Still Spurs came, with Eriksen and Mousa

Dembélé pulling the strings in midfield. On 72 minutes, Spurs won a free kick 25 yards out. Eriksen stood over it, then struck it hard and low towards the right-hand post. Buffon had been expecting a ball over the top of the defensive wall towards the other corner. He was totally wrong-footed. The ball was in the net. And the travelling support at the far end of the ground erupted. This was one of the great performances, against the only other outfit from the top European leagues – the Premier League, the Bundesliga, La Liga, Serie A, and Ligue 1 – that was currently matching the same purple patch Spurs were enjoying. And now, said David Hytner in *The Guardian*, 'Spurs had one foot in the Champions League quarter-finals.'

Unfortunately, they were about to learn there is no substitute for having both feet there. At Wembley, in front of another enormous crowd of 84,010, Spurs went a goal up through Son in the 39th minute. He and Kane were made to regret their wasted chances as Juventus – unlucky not to be awarded a penalty when Vertonghen brought down Douglas Costa – showing their greater maturity by capitalising ruthlessly on two chances as Spurs momentarily switched off. Three minutes into the second half and it was finito. Spurs were done for.

The BBC's Phil McNulty reflected that 'familiar questions will be asked after this devastating loss'. He went on to set out the judgement on Poch and his team as they now stood. 'There is no doubting the quality in this Tottenham side and they were excellent in spells at Wembley, but with two Premier League title campaigns promising so much but unable to deliver and an FA Cup semi-final loss to Chelsea last season, the requirement for tangible success is intensifying.'

At least there would be a third successive Champions League qualification on the horizon to gauge the accuracy of the verdict.

4

Inter Milan v Tottenham Hotspur, 18 September 2018

DESPITE THREE straight wins at the start of the season, including a memorable 3-0 thumping of Manchester United at Old Trafford in which Lucas Moura showed he could do a thing or two in front of goal, the mood was fractious going into Poch's third consecutive Champions League outing.

Spurs launched their campaign with an advertisement provocatively proclaiming the new stadium as 'the only place to watch Champions League football in London' – a clear dig at rivals Arsenal and Chelsea, who faced the long trudge through the Europa League.

Spurs had asked the Premier League to schedule more away fixtures – five of the first seven – at the start of the season. But the new home still wasn't ready. And no one knew when it would be. So Spurs would be back at Wembley, a venue rapidly losing its attraction for the fans, for the 'home' game against Fulham on 18 August. Watford had agreed to reverse their fixture and subsequently ended up victorious at Vicarage Road. Spurs had flagged the home game against Liverpool as the first in the new stadium, but it had to be rescheduled for Wembley because work on the stadium was far from complete. They lost that one as well. So after two successive defeats Spurs were due to open up in Europe away at the San Siro, with the rider that the club confirmed the three Champions League group stage home games would be at Wembley.

Some fans reflected ruefully that intentions rarely turned out as planned, while others – particularly season-ticket and box holders and sponsors – grew steadily more angry at the club's inability to provide any clear information about where they would be playing home games for the rest of the season. Against this disjointed background, another trip to Milan didn't fire the imagination. Spurs didn't sell out their allocation and the campaign was off to a most inauspicious start. There was not the slightest inkling of what was to come.

Pochettino hits out as Inter's last-gasp double sinks Spurs

Matt Law, *Daily Telegraph*, at San Siro

Mauricio Pochettino's cow will certainly not have seen this one coming as Inter Milan staged a late fightback to send Tottenham Hotspur crashing to a third successive defeat for the first time under their manager.

Spurs were heading for a Champions League victory until two late goals left them facing an uphill battle to qualify from a Group B that also includes Barcelona.

Mauro Icardi had been anonymous until he equalised in the 86th minute with an unstoppable volley. And it was from yet another set-piece that Spurs fell to a cruel defeat and had Pochettino's bizarre pre-match cow analogy ringing in the ears of his players.

Pochettino had used a cow failing to comprehend what time a train was due to demonstrate that his team must learn their lessons, but Tottenham fell into the same old trap in Milan.

With two minutes of stoppage-time played, Stefan de Vrij headed a corner back towards goal and Matias Vecino rose highest to nod it past Spurs goalkeeper Michel Vorm and send the San Siro wild.

It was only Inter's second success of the season and questions were inevitably raised about the decision to leave Toby Alderweireld and Kieran Trippier in London, which Pochettino, who had otherwise been calm, bristled at.

'Regrets? Why? Why? Against Watford and Liverpool they [Alderweireld and Trippier] were on the pitch,' said Pochettino. 'What a question. Easy targets. Easy to talk about the players not here. Like Hugo [Lloris] and Dele [Alli] and [Moussa] Sissoko. We need to talk about football.

'You force me to say something not good. You disrespect the players who today showed their quality. Why disrespect them? You can blame me and say you were rubbish gaffer with your selection, but don't blame the people who played.

'Sometimes you ask like you can only play 11. Another 14 are s---, are rubbish, I don't know. It's so easy. I am so disappointed. I respect you a lot. I respect the players.

'You disrespect the players. I don't understand why. Being a player is so difficult. For me it's easier on the touchline. I don't run. It's painful to hear you killing people who give their best.'

Before last night, Spurs had never lost three in a row under Pochettino and the Argentine must now inject confidence into his team following a run of defeats, a string of disappointing performances and Harry Kane's ongoing troubles.

But Pochettino felt Spurs offered encouragement they will quickly improve, saying: 'The most important thing is to be strong and we are strong. We've shown we will be the same as in the past. We have quality.

'Today I start to see good signs that the team is coming back. We showed great personality. We controlled Inter Milan in the San Siro, a difficult place, we showed big character and we were unlucky not to keep the result we deserved. That is my assessment.'

Even without Alderweireld and Trippier, Tottenham should have wrapped this game up after Christian Eriksen had put his team ahead.

Following a first half that Inter had started well, Eriksen scored in the 53rd minute with a slightly fortuitous effort that Samir Handanovic will be disappointed he did not stop. The Inter goalkeeper kept out Eriksen's first effort, but the Dane's second shot rebounded off Miranda and looped over Handanovic, who only managed to palm it back into his net.

Spurs and Pochettino will not have cared how the goal came about, and it gave the visiting side an extra spring in their step.

Kane, despite some industrious running, had squandered the best chance of the game before Eriksen's opener, when he got his feet in a mess in the 37th minute.

It was Eriksen who played a delicious ball over the top of the Inter defence and, when Kane brilliantly rounded Handanovic, there looked to be only one outcome. But the striker could not sort his feet out and the ball dribbled out for a goal-kick. Other than that chance it was Inter who had threatened during the opening 45 minutes. Vorm had to be alert to save from Davinson Sánchez, who headed an Ivan Perisic cross towards his own goal.

But Sánchez made up for that error by cutting out a low cross from Radja Nainggolan that was heading for the waiting Icardi.

Matteo Politano also curled an effort wide after the restart but, following Eriksen's goal, Tottenham should have added to their lead. Érik Lamela was the main culprit as he should have given Handanovic no chance with a shot the keeper saved and failed to find Kane from a superb position in the penalty area.

Pochettino eventually replaced Lamela with Harry Winks, but Tottenham were made to pay a heavy price for the Argentine's misses.

Icardi, making his Champions League debut, had barely had a touch until Kwadwo Asamoah sent over an 86th-minute cross he lashed past Vorm. Then Spurs failed again to deal with a corner and Vecino won the game for Inter.

....

Inter Milan 2 **Tottenham Hotspur 1**

Icardi (85), Vecino (90+2) Eriksen (53)

Inter Milan: Handanovic, Skriniar, de Vrij, Miranda, Asamoah, Vecino, Brozovic, Politano (Keita 72), Nainggolan (Valero 89), Perisic (Candreva 64), Icardi

Unused subs: Padelli, Ranocchia, D'Ambrosio, Berni

Tottenham Hotspur: Vorm, Aurier, Sánchez, Vertonghen, Davies, Dembélé, Dier, Eriksen, Lamela (Winks 72), Son (Lucas Moura 63), Kane (Rose 89)

Unused subs: Gazzaniga, Wanyama, Walker-Peters, Llorente

Attendance: 63,123

....

Many Spurs fans who had opted to watch the game in the pub called it a night early, leaving just as fans of another English side were arriving to see their team start their European campaign in the later televised kick-off. As fans of Spurs and Liverpool passed each other none imagined this was the birth of something that would culminate in a foreign city nine months later.

5

Tottenham Hotspur v Barcelona, 3 October 2018

SPURS HAD racked up two more league wins, mundane affairs away against Brighton and Huddersfield in which they had looked far from convincing, before they returned to European action, the game at Wembley, the visitors Barcelona. It was the marquee match the club would have loved to have staged at the new stadium, but it was not to be.

Wembley fatigue was well and truly setting in amongst fans, but Spurs still opted to charge maximum, category A prices for tickets – from £35 for a seat way up in the gods to £95 for a seat on Level 2. They correctly figured a game against such exalted opposition, with Lionel Messi top of the bill, would always be big box office, and a crowd of over 83,000 proved them right.

For some Spurs fans the pleasure of a still young season was being sapped by the perceived lack of information regarding the new stadium and the way the club had opted to refund fans who had paid up front for their seats in the new ground. While enough turned up to give the evening the required home feel, the number of neutrals along to see Messi and co was notable.

Lionel Messi's masterclass gives Barcelona win over Tottenham

Daniel Taylor, *The Guardian*, at Wembley

For Tottenham it was a harsh lesson in the realities of the Champions League at the highest level. They found out here that it can be frightening at the top and, if anything, they probably got off lightly bearing in mind the long passages when Lionel Messi seemed utterly determined to leave the impression that, in their entire 136-year history, Spurs can never have encountered a man with his powers.

Messi enforced the point by scoring a couple, hitting the post twice in quick succession, playing a key role in

Barcelona's other two goals and menacing his opponents with such brilliance it was bordering on absurd. Nobody should be surprised that panic set into the Spurs defence because, even by Messi's standards, it was difficult to think there could be enough superlatives in existence to cover his mastery. Did Mauricio Pochettino's players show him too much respect? Possibly. But the simple truth is there are times when it seems as though Barcelona's No 10 might just be visiting this planet.

It was certainly not an easy game to work out in light of the 20-minute period at 3-2 when Spurs, against all the odds, might have saved themselves. They were emboldened by goals from Harry Kane and Érik Lamela and there was a prolonged onslaught from the home team before Messi settled it in the 89th minute. The idea, however, that Spurs might have pinched a draw felt almost bewildering given the exhilarating spells when Barça bewitched Wembley and the various points, at 2-0 and 3-1, when it would not have been a surprise if the game turned into a rout. Barça were both brilliant and vulnerable. But they were so superior, overall, that nobody could possibly argue the victory was undeserved. It was merely a surprise they restricted themselves to only four goals.

Spurs will certainly have a better idea now that, with Dele Alli and Christian Eriksen among their absentees, they come up a long way short. Messi's ability to create his own space, a talent he does not relinquish even when he is down to walking speed, made him the central figure and the home team did not get anyone close enough to disturb the rhythm.

It was a masterclass and amid the disappointment of back-to-back Champions League defeats the Spurs supporters must appreciate it was a privilege to see a man taking the sport to its highest levels. This might not be the most beautifully assembled Barça in their modern history but as long as their artillery includes the five-times Ballon d'Or winner they will have the capacity to make even the most proficient opponents question themselves.

At this level, however, Spurs will also have to learn they cannot expect to get very far by defending as obligingly as they did for at least two of the goals. At one point late on Kieran Trippier could be seen arguing with Eric Dier, a substitute, about the chaos in Tottenham's back line. Trippier was one of the players at fault for Barça's final goal and the fit-again Hugo Lloris made a bad decision to leave his goal-line, trying to intercept one of Messi's expertly weighted passes, before Jordi

Alba reached the ball first to set up Philippe Coutinho for the opener, with the goalkeeper stranded and barely 90 seconds on the clock.

Perhaps the credit should go to the Barça attackers for inspiring that kind of trepidation. Luis Suárez may not have scored an away goal in the Champions League since September 2015 but his ability to deceive defenders with his body movement, even without touching the ball sometimes, helped tee up Messi for both his goals. Arthur, another of Barça's Brazilians, also caught the eye and Ivan Rakitic's goal to make it 2-0 was the outstanding moment of a thrilling night.

Rakitic was 25 yards out and the ball was bouncing towards him so high it needed a shot of remarkable control to keep it down. It was a lesson in the art of volleying a ball, a firecracker of a shot that flew through the air, skimmed off the post and speared into the net.

Messi was at the heart of everything and it was difficult not to fear for Spurs, 2-0 down, when a slaloming run at the start of the second half took the Argentinian 40 yards only for his shot to thud against a post. A few minutes later Messi did precisely the same again. He was toying with Spurs and it must have been startling for the home supporters to see the little genius at work. Except that was the point at which the complexion of the evening changed. When Kane created an angle inside the penalty area to fire a splendid shot past the away team's goalkeeper, Marc-André ter Stegen, it felt like a deception that there could be only one goal in it. Perhaps it riled Messi. Three minutes later he picked out Alba on his left. The ball came back his way, Suárez let it go and Messi steered his shot past Lloris.

Still Spurs were not finished. The second half was not even at its midway point when Lamela's shot deflected in off Clément Lenglet. Spurs were also entitled to feel aggrieved that Kane was not awarded a penalty, but it was fitting that Messi was to have the decisive say, rolling the ball past Lloris after some wretched defending in the home ranks. It was true: Spurs have been playing football since 1882 and in all that time, all those thousands of games, they may never have come up against anyone better.

....

Tottenham Hotspur 2   **Barcelona 4**

Kane (52), Lamela (66)   Coutinho (21), Rakitic (28),
                            Messi (56, 90)

Tottenham Hotspur: Lloris, Trippier, Alderweireld, D Sánchez, Davies, Winks, Wanyama (Dier, 57), Moura,

Lamela (Llorente, 79), Son (Sissoko, 66), Kane

Unused subs: Gazzaniga, Rose, Walker-Peters, Skipp

Barcelona: ter Stegen, Nélson Semedo, Piqué, Lenglet, Alba, Arthur (Vidal, 87), Busquets (Vermaelen, 90+1), Rakitic, Messi, Suárez, Coutinho (Rafinha, 83)

Unused subs: D Suárez, Dembélé, Cillessen, El Haddadi

Attendance: 82,137

....

As they made their way home, Spurs fans were left to reflect on the fact that the privilege of seeing a virtuoso performance from one of the greatest players in the history of the game was consolation for the growing disillusionment of this Champions League campaign. Instead they could not put out of their minds the realisation that their team had not only been well-beaten, but also naïve. Naïve in the way they had set up, naïve in the way they had defended, and naïve – perhaps – in falling for some of the gamesmanship the seasoned campaigners of Barcelona had indulged in.

Spurs were supposed to have learned lessons – they weren't new to European competition or to big games against big names. And yet, once again, there were question marks over mental strength and acumen.

The diehards were left to wonder why they'd booked the trip to Eindhoven.

6

PSV Eindhoven v Tottenham Hotspur, 24 October 2018

THE ABILITY to rack up wins in the Premier League while not playing particularly well gave Spurs six more points and the fans hope ahead of the trip to the Netherlands. Eindhoven is a relatively easy trip, accessible by rail, road and air and so demand for tickets was high, despite the requirement to pick tickets up at the stadium before the game with formal photographic ID. (One fan whose ticket was in the name of a female friend turned up in heels, a blonde wig and with two apples shoved down the front of his shirt. He was politely turned away by club staff.)

The club prefer not to sell tickets in this way. It's extra work for them and for the supporters, and for the latter there is always a concern that the process could leave them exposed in hostile cities. Eindhoven isn't the fiercest of destinations, but police intelligence about possible problems with various Dutch and English hooligan groups meant that the requirement to collect tickets at PSV's ground was enforced.

Unsurprisingly there were a higher number of ticket returns than usual, sparking rumours that they had been sold on by some season-ticket holders, the rationale being that these supporters were only interested in the glamour games but had applied for tickets in order to add to their loyalty points that would get them tickets for the more high demand fixtures. While there is undoubtedly some passing on of tickets, many of the faces on European trips are very familiar ones.

The fan experience at the stadium on the night was not what UEFA's slick marketing about its flagship club competition would have you believe. Supporters were subject to long queues and thorough searches on the way in, and the away entrance was set away from the stadium itself, with a bridge over the road and back into the stadium the route by which travelling fans had to enter. It felt, said one, 'as if we were being smuggled in'. Personal items were confiscated at random, including umbrellas on a drizzly night, and coins, that were apparently seen as potential missiles. And yet inside, coins were handed out in change by the refreshment stands. The refreshments themselves would have been overly complimented if they were described as basic. And they weren't cheap.

Once inside the bowl, the general admission away fans stood behind a filthy, scratched, perspex screen behind heavy netting in a corner of the stadium from which it was difficult to see the whole pitch. A view for which they had paid £54 each. Most of the lighting wasn't working and the gradient of the slippery concrete steps was very steep. Those Spurs fans in the UEFA category 1 seats also had cause for complaint as, despite all the emphasis on security, fans of both sides were integrated. It was, one said, 'lairy'. Oh, and then there was the football match...

Spurs hopes hanging by a thread after Lloris red card

Alyson Rudd, *The Times*, Eindhoven

It was thrilling, pulsating and by added time a ragged, desperate mess. It was also the result neither side needed. Tottenham Hotspur's progress in the Champions League hangs by the slenderest of threads after this draw.

It was an outcome that might so easily have been averted had Hugo Lloris not been sent off in the 79th minute. At that juncture Spurs were in control. The France goalkeeper's dismissal gave PSV the shot of adrenaline they needed to find an equaliser after goals from Lucas Moura and Harry Kane had looked to have given Mauricio Pochettino's side a lifeline in the competition. All is not completely lost. Arsenal and Liverpool both progressed in the Champions League after summoning one point from their first three games in 2003 and 2007 respectively but the task facing Tottenham feels insurmountable as they have to somehow wrest points from their remaining games against Inter and Barcelona.

Mark van Bommel had bracketed Spurs alongside those two sides but, in truth, Pochettino's team are far less capable of taking and sustaining control, of killing off their opponents' spirit. When Christian Eriksen spoke of the team throwing the game away, it was not an exaggeration. Spurs could see salvation but, with ten minutes to go, relinquished the chance of it.

Van Bommel had also painted his side as the underdogs but there was little chance PSV, all-conquering so far domestically, were about to become wallflowers and from the start both Gastón Pereiro and Hirving Lozano's neat control at pace was a problem for the visitors.

Lozano was 'exceptional' according to his manager, who, when asked if he would be able to keep hold of the Mexico international, smiled ruefully and said he was glad he was part of his squad right now. It was Lozano whom Lloris fouled for his red card. It was Lozano who kept plugging away when his team-mates wilted. It was Lozano who stole a show Tottenham were supposed to star in and thereby revitalise their European adventure. Instead, Pochettino's team were a frustrating mix of Premier League pedigree and naivety.

The signs that Lozano would become a problem were there from the start and Mousa Dembélé became irate when the player known as Chucky fell easily under his challenge. Dembélé had his head in his hands when cautioned for dealing with the next Lozano run he faced. From the subsequent free kick, Pereiro hit the side-netting. This was not about to become a one-sided affair, not unless Spurs believed in their superior attributes, and slowly they did.

The first save of note came as a consequence of a strike from Kane. His effort added some urgency to the Spurs performance and the England striker hit the bar soon afterwards.

PSV refused to be cowed by Spurs' composure and goal threat. This was a game to be won, not navigated, and they made the most of a mistake by Toby Alderweireld to take the lead. Alderweireld let Lozano steal the ball, gallop towards goal and loop the ball in off the defender's challenge past Lloris. The goal provided a particularly delightful piece of schadenfreude for the home fans given that Alderweireld began his career at Ajax, their rivals. They also enjoyed the fact that Davinson Sánchez thought he had equalised only for the assistant referee to flag for offside.

Their luck ran out when Kieran Trippier pulled the ball back for Moura to beat Jeroen Zoet.

Still, the Dutch champions refused to retreat. Pereiro hit the woodwork with a rasping effort and as the half-time whistle sounded, Van Bommel's side were looking busy, eager and almost impatient to attack again.

Spurs were first out for the second half, however, and improved their levels of intensity, with Eriksen forcing an excellent save from Zoet before Kane gave the visitors the lead as he reached a beautiful cross from Eriksen. The previous evening Pochettino had said that he was unsure if he would start Eriksen as he recovered from injury but it was the Dane, making his first start since September 22, who consistently gave Tottenham their classy edge.

Son Heung-min and Dembélé both attempted shots from outside the area while Lozano increasingly became PSV's most incisive player.

Son's sprightly approach had been preferred to Érik Lamela, a player in form but who struggles with the relentlessness of Spurs' itinerary because of a hip injury, but Lamela, inevitably, came off the bench and, with his first chance, struck the crossbar.

As PSV tired, a third goal for Spurs felt inevitable. They were not quite coasting but were the team with energy and verve and imagination. Instead, Lloris was sent off for the second time in his career, after clattering into Lozano and Michel Vorm saved the resultant free kick from the edge of the area.

Van Bommel's side were buoyed by the red card all the same and the balance of power shifted, allowing Luuk de Jong to stab home an equaliser from close range.

© The Times/News Licensing

....

PSV Eindhoven 2 **Tottenham Hotspur 2**

Lozano (29), de Jong (87) Lucas Moura (39), Kane (54)

PSV Eindhoven: Zoet, Dumfries, Schwaab, Viergever, Angelino, Rosario, Hendrix, Lozano, Pereiro (Gakpo 83), Malen, de Jong

Unused subs: Isimit-Mirin, Behich, Room, Sainsbury, Ramselaar, Gutiérrez

Tottenham Hotspur: Lloris, Trippier, Alderweireld, D Sánchez, Davies, Dier, Dembélé (Winks 74), Lucas Moura (Lamela 64), Eriksen, Son (Vorm 81), Kane

Unused subs: Wanyama, Sissoko, Llorente, Aurier

Attendance 35,000

....

After the game, away fans were held back for even longer than the veterans of European trips were wearily accustomed to. A good hour after the final whistle, they were allowed to leave the ground under the watch of surly and aggressive police. Those who didn't need to head back to the main station had to risk, at best, more aggression when they tried to explain that they had another route home. Those that made it back into town to see if there were any bars still open after midnight had scant chance to reflect on a campaign that looked all but over. The glamour, the glamour, of it all.

7

Tottenham Hotspur v PSV Eindhoven, 6 November 2018

BY LATE October, few believed Spurs would be moving into the new stadium any time soon. A high-profile game against high-flying Manchester City was yet another casualty of the delay. Sky's understandable insistence on broadcasting the game live and Wembley's commitment to an NFL match on the scheduled weekend meant that for fans of either side there was very little time to make proper plans, the game having been switched to a Monday night. Spurs were not endearing themselves to anyone.

A 1-0 defeat in that game underlined the gap between Spurs and the kind of squad that could compete seriously for titles – although for all City's elan it can be hard to ignore the wealth that being owned by a nation state brings.

Following a League Cup win against West Ham, and a fortunate 3-2 result away at Wolves at the start of November, Spurs returned to Wembley for a must-win game against PSV Eindhoven. Just over 46,500 turned up, a reflection of discontent with the venue, the match pricing, and the campaign itself. The media reported that a capped capacity to adhere to Brent Council's restriction on the limited number of 90,000 capacity games permitted was a contributory cause. Curiously, this only came to light after the match, with visiting PSV fans taking double the number of away tickets that would have been made available under UEFA rules of a 51,000-capacity cap.

Matters were at a low ebb, and the booing that greeted Poch's decision to take off Lucas Moura and replace him with Érik Lamela was a rare show of displeasure from the crowd towards the manager. European glory seemed a distant pleasure. And then, as he so often does, Harry Kane stepped up to give Spurs the first lifeline in what would turn out to be an extraordinary sequence of them.

Kane's late show keeps Spurs' slim hopes alive

Sam Wallace, *Daily Telegraph*, at Wembley

There is still a mountain to climb for Tottenham Hotspur to survive in the Champions League beyond next month, but when Harry Kane can win a game in the space of 11 minutes, perhaps it is not so implausible that they could somehow find a way to get through.

There have been some great nights for Kane at Wembley over the course of his remarkable goalscoring career and, although this one was not among the classics, it lived up to the usual drama around the England captain. He scored twice in the closing stages, the second a twice-deflected header that may yet be chalked up as an own goal, to make Spurs' daunting task to reach the second round just that little more feasible.

They still have to earn major results in their final two games, starting with a win over Inter Milan at Wembley on Nov 28. 'You know me,' Mauricio Pochettino said afterwards, 'I'm so optimistic.'

It would be fair to say he did not look very optimistic until Kane's 78th-minute equaliser, after what seemed an eternity chasing Luuk de Jong's opener after 61 seconds.

Pochettino will need all his optimism for Spurs' final Champions League group match on Dec 11.

That will be when – depending on whether they beat Inter and if so by how many – Spurs must better or match the Italians' result against PSV in their final game. Spurs will have to do so away to Barcelona who, despite being held to a 1-1 draw with a late equaliser in Milan, have secured qualification for the knockout rounds. It will be difficult if, in the Nou Camp, Spurs again concede another early goal. But with Kane in the side, Pochettino has reason to hope – and overall this was not a poor performance.

It was a strange atmosphere, an evening on which Spurs' support was largely subdued, although they did boo Pochettino's decision to replace Lucas Moura in the second half. The Spurs manager made light of it, although it feels like the Wembley holiday mood is waning among the Spurs fans and the pitch was once again well below standard.

Asked whether the playing surface was a factor, Mark van Bommel, the PSV manager, replied, 'No, it's s---', as if to say that it was no worse than he had expected.

It had been a night of scrapping for Kane, seeking out the occasional chances that came his way. He hunted down his two goalscoring chances, the first of which, Pochettino pointed out, was made for him with a knock-down from Fernando Llorente, one of the second-half substitutes.

That was an instinctive finish when the ball dropped, the second a header that took two deflections before it rolled into the corner of the PSV goal – but then there is always a chance Kane will be the right man in the right place at the right time. He has 13 goals in 14 Champions League games for Spurs and these next two games are when his side will need him more than ever – especially if they keep conceding so cheaply.

It was already a bad night for Spurs with 61 seconds played, when a corner won early by PSV's 21-year-old Spanish full-back Angelino was nodded firmly past Paulo Gazzaniga by De Jong. The visitors were just that much sharper – Dele Alli adroitly blocked from following his man in the area by the run of centre-back Nick Viergever, a nicely executed move.

On the touchline, Pochettino had the whole game to reflect on his team's weakness defending set-pieces, a problem that had surfaced earlier in the season and in particular the defeat by Watford.

Spurs recovered and created enough chances to score in the first half. They finished the game with 75 per cent possession. They should never have allowed themselves to be behind in the first place.

PSV have 11 victories from 11 Eredivisie games, although in the first half it was their goalkeeper Jeroen Zoet who was their outstanding performer. He stopped two efforts in quick succession from Alli and Christian Eriksen, when it seemed all either needed to do was to direct their attempts fractionally away from Zoet, who stood his ground.

Pochettino had picked an attacking side with a front three of Kane, Son Heung-min and Moura, supported by Alli. He left it until just after the hour when he finally went for the change. It was Moura, who had embarked on one first-half run that had taken him past four opponents before he was finally stopped by centre-back Daniel Schwaab.

A section of the 41,500 home fans, who had made considerably less noise than their Dutch counterparts, booed the decision.

Érik Lamela took his place and later Llorente, for Son, and Kieran Trippier, as a replacement for Serge Aurier, would also come on. Spurs' possession count had been overwhelming. Aside from Gazzaniga electing to Cruyff-turn his way out of the pressure applied by PSV's striker Hirving Lozano, there had been no moments of anxiety in the second half before the Kane goals.

Finally, Kane swung a left boot at Llorente's knock-down and connected cleanly enough to dispatch his shot past Zoet. His winner came from a back-post cross from Ben Davies and a downward header that struck Viergever and then substitute Trent Sainsbury before dropping in the corner of Zoet's goal.

It had been a long and hard fight, with 30 attempts on the PSV goal. But Spurs are still alive in the competition, however tough the task ahead.

....

Tottenham Hotspur 2   PSV Eindhoven 1
Kane (78, 89)   de Jong (2)

Tottenham Hotspur: Gazzaniga, Aurier (Trippier 75), Alderweireld, D Sánchez, Davies, Winks, Eriksen, Lucas Moura (Lamela 62), Alli, Son (Llorente 75), Kane
Unused subs: Vorm, Walker-Peters, Sissoko, Skipp

PSV Eindhoven: Zoet, Dumfries, Schwaab, Viergever, Angelino, Rosario, Hendrix, Lozano, Pereiro (Malen 73), Bergwijn (Gutiérrez 86), de Jong (Sainsbury 81)
Unused subs: Behich, Room, Ramselaar, Mauro Júnior
Attendance: 46,588

Conversation on the way home and in the queues for the trains that were blessedly shorter than usual because of the relatively low crowd – that Wembley fatigue was never far away – was at last positive; if only a touch. Implausibly, given their showing so far, Spurs were still in with a chance. And they had Harry Kane, who was proving to be not only one of the finest natural goalscorers seen in a Lilywhite shirt for many a year, but also an increasingly inspirational figure. A third game in seven days, away at Crystal Palace, was next, and then the international break.

8

Tottenham Hotspur v Inter Milan, 28 November 2018

BUOYED BY a 3-1 victory against Chelsea at Wembley a few days before, a game in which Tottenham's high-tempo and skilful approach brought back memories of the best of Poch's sides from the previous three years, Spurs faced yet another must-win game.

The crowd was up on the PSV game, just over 57,000 – a decent turnout but 40% lower in comparison to the vast attendances of the previous season. The number of Inter fans in home areas led to several blocks being dubbed 'Little Italy' and resulted in some lively exchanges in the stands.

It turned out to be a nervy, nervy night. The Italians defended competently as the best Italian sides are wont to do, and they always looked smart enough to produce something to test Spurs, too. Nerves subdued the crowd, and the tension threatened to spill onto the pitch, with Spurs looking increasingly likely to concede.

Christian Eriksen pounces to give Spurs crucial victory over Internazionale

David Hytner, *The Guardian*, at Wembley

Tottenham had to win and, as the second-half minutes ticked down and Wembley grew increasingly fraught, they came to crave a single chance; a shot at Champions League salvation.

Internazionale had been obdurate and it was difficult to remember Spurs creating anything in open play after the interval. Was this the slow death of their hopes? One thing was plain: Mauricio Pochettino and his players needed something special.

In one of those rare moments of perfect clarity, they got it. There were 80 minutes on the clock when the rejuvenated Moussa Sissoko drove forward and Inter defenders were drawn towards him; their defensive structure finally punctured.

Sissoko fed the ball square to Dele Alli and, suddenly, it was on. Alli had Christian Eriksen on the overlap, easing into space, and he teed him up, having taken a touch as he pivoted. Eriksen had entered as a substitute only 10 minutes earlier but he did not feel his heart race. With great composure, he lifted a beautiful first-time finish past Samir Handanovic.

It is at such moments, when the pressure is at its most acute, that the big players deliver. Sissoko, Alli and Eriksen combined to do just that and 1-0 was the dream scoreline for Spurs because it took them above Inter into second place in Group B on the first tie-breaker criterion – the head-to-head record between the clubs. The fixture at San Siro ended in a 2-1 Inter win but the away goal that Eriksen scored that night now stands to count double.

Spurs still have it all to do, however. Inter will be the favourites to beat PSV Eindhoven at home in the final round of matches and, in that event, the London club will need to win against Barcelona at the Camp Nou. In short, they must match Inter's result. Barcelona are already assured of finishing on top of the section. Might they rest players? To Spurs's delight, however, they are alive and in control of their destiny.

Pochettino had spoken beforehand about his relish for seemingly impossible missions and the key to this one was always going to be the players' attitude. They had shown it in the previous tie at home to PSV, when a pair of late Harry Kane goals swept them to a 2-1 win, and they kept their cool once more.

Inter are a better team than PSV and they bristled with latent menace on the break. Moreover, they were defensively disciplined and there were plenty of times when Spurs looked up to see a wall of black and blue. From the outset, it was clear that unpicking them and striking the right balance between pushing but not over-committing would be tough.

Spurs pressed onto the front foot while Inter were happy to counterpunch and it was tight and edgy. If the home team needed any reminding of how Inter could fashion something out of nothing, it came on 27 minutes when Ivan Perisic released Mauro Icardi. The striker had the legs on Toby Alderweireld and the Tottenham defender knew it. He took the yellow card with a cynical foul.

Moments earlier, Harry Winks had put Hugo Lloris in trouble with a loose backpass and the goalkeeper got away with an even looser ball, which had been intended for Alderweireld. Serge Aurier would also win a vital challenge on the substitute Borja Valero inside the area at the end of the first half. Spurs' margin for error was slim to nonexistent. They had been pepped by Saturday's 3-1 win over Chelsea, when they tore into their opponents from the first whistle, but there was a different approach here and a different feel, a different tempo.

Against Chelsea, Pochettino had played Alli in the space behind two strikers but on this occasion, the England international's starting position was nominally to the left of a midfield trio. As ever, he had the licence to bomb forward, to roam in between the lines.

Pochettino started Winks rather than Eric Dier in front of the back four and he brought energy and assurance in possession while Sissoko supplied the power. His transformation from expensive misfit to driving force continues apace. Pochettino had raised eyebrows by omitting Eriksen from the starting XI and it feels as though he is managing the player's fitness amid concerns about an abdominal problem. Eriksen would eventually cause pain to Inter's gut.

Spurs struggled to get in behind their opponents in the first half but they still had their moments, none better than when Winks shaped a right-footed curler against the crossbar from 20 yards. Lucas Moura had shouted in vain for an early penalty after Matteo Politano unwisely dangled in a leg on him – it would have been a brave award from the referee Cüneyt Cakir – while Kane laid on an opening for Alli only for his teammate to lift high. Lucas shot too close to Handanovic after a thrust from Sissoko.

The anxiety among the majority in the 57,132 crowd was palpable and the longer it remained goalless, the better it suited Inter; they came to threaten more in the second half as the spaces opened up.

Pochettino introduced Son Heung-min and Eriksen and the latter's first touch was a free-kick that Jan Vertonghen might have converted at the far post. Lloris saved smartly from Perisic and, after the goal, from Danilo D'Ambrosio while the final action saw Kwadwo Asamoah unleash a goalbound drive that Alderweireld blocked. Spurs will travel to Barcelona in hope.

© Guardian News & Media

Tottenham Hotspur 1   Inter Milan 0
Eriksen (80)
Tottenham Hotspur: Lloris, Aurier, Alderweireld, Vertonghen, Davies, Sissoko, Winks (Dier 87), Lucas Moura (Son 62), Alli, Lamela (Eriksen 70), Kane

Unused subs: Gazzaniga, Rose, Walker-Peters, Llorente

Inter Milan: Handanovic, D'Ambrosio, Skriniar, de Vrij (Miranda 82), Asamoah, Vecino, Brozovic, Politano (Keita 83), Nainggolan (Valero 44), Perisic, Icardi

Unused subs: Padelli, Martinez, Ranocchia, Berni, Candreva

Attendance: 57,132

Once again on the brink of elimination, what had seemed to be shaping up as a miserable season suddenly looked as if it might have some saving graces.

Now Spurs needed to match Inter's result in the toughest of places; at the Noucamp against Barcelona. The trip so many had been waiting for.

9

Barcelona v Tottenham Hotspur, 11 December 2018

WHEN THE group stage draw was held in Monaco back in August, Barcelona was the top team most wanted from Pot 1 and was the trip everyone wanted to make. One of Europe's great cities, and a ground that Spurs had not played at for many years. The savings made from not going to Milan and choosing a berth in front of a TV were eagerly drawn on.

While the city, barring the pickpocketing and bag theft, offers plenty, the experience at the stadium underlined once again why seasoned travellers to European games are beginning to question whether it's worth it. There had been reports of excessive force being used by security personnel at the Nou

Camp when English, Dutch and German clubs had been visited previously. But nothing prepared Spurs fans for what they were about to undergo. Just hours before kick-off, the entrance plans – arranged weeks before between both clubs and local police – were inexplicably changed without any communication to fans or fan groups. Fans were made to walk all around the stadium and then channelled through a narrow gap in a fence before being held in a confined space outside the turnstiles.

At one stage, as the fans were funnelled through in small groups, they were set upon by masked security staff with batons. Limbs were broken, heads were cut … one fan was so badly beaten he was left unable to work for months afterwards.

Once inside the ground, the Spurs fans were directed to the very top level of the stadium and into the most basic of areas. Entry to toilets and facilities were frequently blocked by overly aggressive security staff. Fans were attacked in their seats – videos later confirmed that the assaults had been unprovoked. All this with tickets the most expensive of the entire campaign at £62 each – higher, it would transpire, than the entry level price for the final itself! It is little wonder that Barcelona frequently rank bottom of surveys for fan experience across Europe.

Lucas Moura's strike helps Spurs to complete miracle

Sam Wallace, *Daily Telegraph*, at the Nou Camp

This turned out to be the miracle of Barcelona for Mauricio Pochettino's team, with a place in the Champions League round of 16 against all the odds, even if the real drama took place in Milan where an improbable draw for PSV Eindhoven secured Spurs' progress.

Against a Barcelona team that rested many of its biggest names – although Lionel Messi was on the pitch for the final 30 minutes or so – the Tottenham Hotspur substitute Lucas Moura scored an equaliser that salvaged the draw for his team, and a place in the knockout stages. But really a draw in the Nou Camp should never have been enough for Spurs when the night began.

Instead, this was a colossal cock-up by Inter Milan, who failed to beat PSV, the last-placed team in Group B, in their own stadium. Only the second point of the Champions League group for the Dutch champions meant that Spurs' draw was enough to see them through in second place on the head-to-head between them and the Italian club.

Perhaps the new White Hart Lane will see Champions League football this season after all. Spurs came back from a wonderful goal from Ousmane Dembélé in the seventh minute which might have drained their belief. They had to face Messi in a nerve-racking end to the game, but although there were moments when he spun and passed and moved this was Messi in third gear, not top speed.

There were eight changes from the Barcelona team that dispatched Espanyol at the weekend. In the place of the likes of Gerard Piqué, Luis Suárez and Jordi Alba, came a team of relative youth and some inexperience but all suffused with that old Barça magic. There was a Champions League debut for the academy graduate Carles Aleñá, a 20-year-old Catalan who stroked the ball around in the centre of midfield as so many of his predecessors have done. At left-back there was a start for the 18-year-old Juan Miranda, and complementing that were some experienced faces too.

Philippe Coutinho, only a substitute in the win over Espanyol, started in attack. The Portuguese right-back

Nelson Semedo stayed in the team and on the right wing was Dembélé.

The 21-year-old Frenchman is one month younger than Kyle Walker-Peters, who was starting his first Champions League game for Spurs and will never forget the moment that Moussa Sissoko's ropy header came at him.

It was a horrible moment for Walker-Peters who, on another day and in another game would have brought the awkward bouncing ball down and distributed it without any trouble. But now he was in the crosshairs of Dembélé who is mesmerisingly quick, so quick there is a kind of cruelty at the way in which he makes fast players look slow and slow players look static.

He did the same to Kyle Walker playing for France in Paris last year and now it was another player of much the same name to suffer the same fate. Dembélé first forced Walker-Peters off the ball, and then pushed it into an area where the Spurs man had to twist and chase. That was when the jets went on and having seen Dembélé over one shoulder, Walker-Peters was now watching him over another.

Dembélé is not just quick, he was on this occasion a brilliantly ruthless finisher. He shaped to strike with his right and Harry Winks, running back to cover, had to gamble on that being the shot.

He launched himself in front of the ball and was still sliding towards the corner flag when Dembélé did the switch onto his left foot and slotted it past Hugo Lloris.

A breathtaking goal, and it took Spurs a while to regain their composure.

Naturally, they had to contend with Barcelona having a lot of the ball and the full press was not always wise with Dembélé and Coutinho out wide and very dangerous. They had conceded from a move that began when Barcelona were defending a free-kick. With PSV Eindhoven winning against Inter Milan there was no onus on them to throw everything to attack and their best first half chances were when they won the ball and attacked quickly.

Both were made by Christian Eriksen. He slipped in Danny Rose down the left for a cross that Heung-min Son could not quite reach. The Spurs striker should have done better with the second, holding off Thomas Vermaelen for a shot that Jasper Cillessen saved with his feet. It could have been worse for Spurs at half-time, with Coutinho having clipped a post with a shot he took deceptively early.

Valverde took Rakitic off at half-time and, in his place, came Sergio Busquets. In those opening periods of the first half, Spurs played higher up the pitch and asked a few more questions of Barcelona.

They created some openings and the best of those fell to Harry Kane, who snatched at his shot and got under it, flaying it high and wide.

There were goals to be had for Spurs, and Barcelona were not so much of a threat in the first part of the second half. ÉrikLamela was brought on for Walker-Peters after the hour and then out on the touchline the crowd stirred as another Argentine broke away from the players warming up and went to the dugout to remove his tracksuit.

That was Messi, who came on with 26 minutes left and was handed the captain's armband then being worn by Busquets and did little for the next 15 minutes.

The news of a goal for Inter Milan came with about 17 minutes of regulation time left at the Nou Camp where the game had gone flat and the home team seemed to be losing interest. At right-back now, Sissoko put a cross to the back post where Lucas Moura, on for Son, fluffed his header.

It was Kane who made the goal in the end, crossing from the left wing to Moura arriving in the area as

Spurs pressed attackers forward. They might have had a second from Danny Rose later on but as Inter faltered, it was enough.

....

Barcelona 1   Tottenham Hotspur 1

Dembélé (7)   Lucas Moura (85)

Barcelona: Cillessen, Nélson Semedo, Lenglet, Vermaelen, Miranda, Aleñá, Rakitic (Busquets 45), Arthur, Dembélé (D Suárez 76), El Haddadi (Messi 63), Coutinho

Unused subs: ter Stegen, Piqué, Alba, Vidal

Tottenham Hotspur: Lloris, Walker-Peters (Lamela 61), Alderweireld, Vertonghen, Rose, Winks (Llorente 83), Sissoko, Eriksen, Alli, Kane, Son (Lucas Moura 71)

Unused subs: Gazzaniga, Dier, Davies, Skipp

Attendance: 69,961

....

As the game neared its conclusion, noting the massing of police and security guards at the exits, many fans opted to leave to avoid yet more trouble. They thus missed the moment when Lucas Moura secured their team's passage to the knockout stages.

Those who remained to celebrate wildly were kept back for almost an hour and exited the ground to find the metro had closed. It was a 6km walk back into town.

Barcelona were later fined a paltry €20,000 by UEFA for 'insufficient organisation'; a sanction both Tottenham Hotspur and the Supporters' Trust condemned as derisory. However, it is worth noting this was the first occasion a club had faced punishment for crowd control, so this was a tiny step forward for UEFA. And the fact that the club itself had added its voice to the concerns over the treatment of Spurs supporters was also a milestone. The clubs usually prefer not to say anything, not to rock the boat. But enough, it seemed, was enough, and the Spurs board deserve credit for speaking out.

More than a few fans said after the game they would never return, with others questioning whether travelling to European games was something they were prepared to continue doing. For the fans present, what should have been a great night was soured by the treatment they had been subjected to. Even so, few could disguise their pleasure at having come back from the brink a third time to secure passage to the knockout phase. What's more, despite the appalling treatment handed out to them, Spurs' fans were impeccably behaved.

Such an observation often draws the response 'so they should be, what of it?', but when complaints about the routine poor treatment of English club fans abroad are so often brushed away with casual reference to stories of incidents long past, it is important to make the point.

10

Tottenham Hotspur v Borussia Dortmund, 13 February 2019

AFTER A winning run through December, home losses to Wolves and Manchester United at the turn of the year saw Spurs fall off the blistering pace being set in the Premier League by Manchester City and Liverpool. Further, they were now without injured Harry Kane when the Champions League recommenced in February.

With the stadium saga still seemingly interminable, Wembley was again the venue. Dortmund were by now familiar opponents, also though with injury problems of their own. Still, a crowd of 71,000 was healthy enough, and they were treated to a display that suggested Poch's men had taken on board the harsh lessons they had absorbed along the way. As always, the Dortmund fans brought much colour and much noise with their choreographed support, drums and flags.

Son Heung-min and Jan Vertonghen shine in thumping CL win

Miguel Delaney, *The Independent*, Wembley

Tottenham Hotspur get so close to the next round and, maybe, the next level. Mauricio Pochettino's side effectively did to Borussia Dortmund what clubs like Juventus have done to them in the Champions League, and so maturely picked them off for a fine 3-0 win. It only added to this perception that the manager's big tactical decision paid off, and proved one of the decisive factors in a match that involved so many decisive players from both sides out injured. Jan Vertonghen was surprisingly placed at wing-back and, after an initial struggle, pretty much won the game – and then the tie – with an assist and then the second goal. The identity of who he crossed for with the first goal was pointed, though, because it showed that not all of the decisive players were out. Son Heung-min has actually gone beyond decisive, to the verges of world-class. He set Spurs on their way, lifting them to a higher level, by lifting himself for that tidiest of volleys. Fernando Llorente then finished the game, and all but finished the job, with a fine header.

It was just such a polished team display in general, as they showed an accumulated maturity beyond Dortmund. Whether that is enough to now beat the best sides remains to be seen, but this performance should mean we see it played out this season, such was the extent of Spurs' lead. It would be remarkable if this tie was turned over, such was the gulf.

Spurs just so damningly reminded Dortmund of their youth, and injuries. The German side just didn't look like Bundesliga leaders, but did look like a side missing some of their best players.

Their most promising players, meanwhile, didn't really ignite.

It had been a stand-offish game, occasionally lifted by the forwards willing to take a stride forward, and that was usually the livewire Sancho. Some of his runs were, quite simply, what you watch football for. One moment that saw him turn Davinson Sánchez one way then the other was particularly wondrous.

His runs aren't necessarily how you win football, though, because they were still just lacking that end product. That is natural for a player of that age, and particularly in a Dortmund team missing its players that most provide end product: Paco Alcácer and Marco Reus.

Christian Pulisic did occasionally look dangerous, but he was still mostly functional straight lines to Sancho's unpredictable squiggles. That was never truer than when he squandered a huge chance on 62 minutes, essentially by continuing to just run.

He was only in the team because of injuries, and his performance reflected what has been a somewhat underwhelming performance level of late. Sánchez had the measure of him, in a way he didn't with Sancho. He will need a recharge for when he joins Chelsea.

This was also the difference. Dortmund just lacked the end product of someone like Son.

His ability to conjure something out of nothing is what is making him an increasingly revered player, and influential one.

Spurs hadn't quite done nothing here but, other than one supreme Lucas Moura touch-and-volley, they had mostly been contained. It was time for the release, the trap having been set. They just had to get Son on the ball. The latter was what Jan Vertonghen did superbly with that exquisite cross, but it still needed to be finished. Son did that exquisitely, combining elegance, accuracy and enough power. The delightful volley left Roman Bürki with no chance, although the defence in front of him had given Son plenty of space.

Spurs were now fully in control, as was the vibrant Vertonghen as he launched himself at a Serge Aurier cross for the second.

Dortmund were by now all over the place, and predictably succumbed to one of their main flaws: problems at set-pieces. There was Llorente to take advantage, and give his side what feels an insurmountable advantage for the second leg.

© The Independent

....

Tottenham Hotspur 3　Borussia Dortmund 0
Son (47), Vertonghen (83), Llorente (86)

Tottenham Hotspur: Lloris, Foyth, D Sánchez, Alderweireld, Aurier, Sissoko (Wanyama 90+1), Winks, Vertonghen, Eriksen, Son (Lamela 90), Lucas Moura (Llorente 84)
Unused subs: Gazzaniga, Trippier, Rose, Skipp

Borussia Dortmund: Bürki, Hakimi, Toprak, Zagadou (Schmelzer 77), Diallo, Dahoud, Witsel, Delaney, Sancho (Guerreiro 88), Götze, Pulisic (Bruun Larsen 88)

Unused subs: Balerdi, Philipp, Wolf, Hitz

Attendance 71,214

....

Less swashbuckling than in some of the most exhilarating games under Poch, Spurs were nonetheless very good to watch. But they also demonstrated a maturity in controlling the game and striking ruthlessly when they could. Utterly in control from start to finish, the team had the stands jumping in a way few could have thought likely just weeks before.

Jan Vertonghen had delivered one of the great European performances, one all the more remarkable because he was deployed as a wing-back. It was his perfectly executed cross that made Son's goal. And that goal, a thing of beauty, cushioned on the volley into the back of the net from just outside the six-yard box – an incredibly difficult finish made to look easy. It came on 47 minutes, and relieved some of the pressure that was starting to build after a goalless first half. To produce the football that Spurs did in that second half was a demonstration of mental strength that is the sign of a top-class team.

11

Borussia Dortmund v Tottenham Hotspur, 5 March 2019

SPURS HAVE played in Dortmund three times in the past four campaigns, so for the many thousands of fans who travelled it really was familiar territory. So much so that, on the Alter Markt in the centre of town, a ball stuck in scaffolding from a game of street football during the Europa League game in March 2016 had been pinned ceremoniously to the now scaffolding-free building by the locals.

There were worries about the team's form after a meek away loss at Burnley, a comprehensive defeat at Stamford Bridge and a disappointing derby draw, at

Wembley, against Arsenal. The standing joke among the travelling support in Dortmund was that you weren't really a Spurs fan if you hadn't seriously contemplated losing this one 4-3.

Harry Kane's deadly artistry fires Spurs past Dortmund and into last eight

David Hytner, *The Guardian*, Signal Iduna Park

It is perhaps worth recalling the situation in which Tottenham found themselves after the third match of this Champions League group phase. With only one point on the board, even Mauricio Pochettino had practically written them off. 'It's nearly over,' the manager said. 'It will be very difficult.'

Look at Spurs now. Their ride into the last 16 came complete with white knuckles but what underpinned their progress to the quarter-final – on a memorable night at the home of the Bundesliga leaders – was calmness and conviction. There were anxious moments in a first-half that Borussia Dortmund dominated but with Jan Vertonghen imperious in central defence and Hugo Lloris making a couple of excellent saves as well as several decent ones, they kept the home side at bay.

The worry had been that one Dortmund goal would set the alarm bells ringing after Spurs set out to protect a 3-0 first-leg lead. It did not happen. And when Harry Kane ran through on goal after 49 minutes to display his world-class finishing touch, Pochettino's team could coast into the last eight of Europe's elite club competition for only the third time in their history.

Kane's nerveless effort also took him to the top of Spurs's all-time European scoring list with 24 goals. He has 14 in 17 Champions League games, too – a phenomenal ratio that bears comparison with the very best.

This was a perfectly executed away-day number, a performance to advertise the steelier mentality which Pochettino has instilled in his squad. The sound of silence from the Dortmund crowd for most of the second half was a thing of beauty for the Spurs players.

The first half was always going to be pivotal and when Tottenham reached the interval with the score intact, it seemed as though they had completed the lion's share of their task. Dortmund had gone for it, after all.

Lucien Favre had omitted Thomas Delaney, the central midfielder, in order to accommodate Paco

Alcácer and Mario Götze in the starting lineup. Götze roamed alongside Marco Reus in the central attacking areas, behind Alcácer, and Reus in particular bristled with menace.

Dortmund pressed high from the first whistle, swarming all over Spurs, and they struggled to get out of their half. The first-half was a siege, a time for Pochettino's defenders to prove themselves in the face of wave after wave of attacks from the home side.

The manager's 5-3-2 system looked a little narrow and he would ask Son Heung-min to move to the left flank towards the end of the first-half and Christian Eriksen to go to the right.

This was a different way for Spurs to win, too. They played deeper than usual and enjoyed only 35% possession. But Pochettino could be delighted at how his players dug in.

Vertonghen set the tone that the manager had asked for with a magnificent saving tackle to deny Reus on 11 minutes, after Davinson Sánchez had erred to allow him in. Reus looked set to punish Spurs only for the Belgian to stretch into a perfectly timed sliding challenge.

The atmosphere pulsed and the Yellow Wall – the vast single tier behind one of the goals – really was something to behold; a reminder of Dortmund's scale. Spurs have based one end of their new stadium on it. And as an aside, the ovation that the diehards on the Yellow Wall gave to their players after the full-time whistle was a demonstration of their class.

Dortmund took risks and they pushed, straining for the early goal that would have put a different slant on the match. Spurs suffered. But they resisted. Or, more precisely, Lloris resisted. The goalkeeper made five saves between the midway point and the interval, with two of them classics – the first from Julian Weigl's glancing header, the second from Götze's curler. Lloris, who also would deny Alcácer at the very end, now has 100 clean sheets for the club.

Spurs had one chance in the first-half but it was a big one. Eriksen's 31st-minute pass released Son but, one on one with Roman Bürki, he prodded wide of the near post with his right foot. Should he have taken it on with his left? What incensed Spurs was the nudge that the chasing Marius Wolf gave to Son. The referee, Danny Makkelie, felt there was not enough in it, which spared Dortmund the concession of a penalty.

It did not matter. When Spurs fashioned their next chance, early in the second half, it fell to the player that Pochettino would have chosen. Dortmund only half-cleared a Spurs thrust and it was Moussa Sissoko who released Kane with a slide-rule pass. The club's most lethal finisher had only Bürki to beat and he had the time.

Kane weighed up the situation in a heartbeat, calibrating the angles and the closeness of the chasing defence. Then he finished, putting a little lift on the right-foot shot to make it all the harder for Bürki. When the ball hit the net, the tie was over.

Dortmund's build-up play had been slick in the first-half, the danger they created palpable, but they lacked ruthlessness in front of goal. Kane, by contrast, had scored with his first sniff of an opening. It is a detail that bodes well for the quarter-finals.

Spurs have come a long way. It is where they intend to go that brings the excitement.

© Guardian News & Media

....

Borussia Dortmund 0   Tottenham Hotspur 1

Kane (48)

Borussia Dortmund: Bürki, Wolf (Bruun Larsen 88), Weigl, Akanji, Diallo, Witsel, Sancho, Götze, Reus (Delaney 74), Guerreiro (Pulisic 62), Alcácer

Unused subs: Hakimi, Zagadou, Schmelzer, Hitz

Tottenham Hotspur: Lloris, Alderweireld, D Sánchez, Vertonghen, Aurier, Sissoko, Winks (Dier 55), Eriksen (Rose 83), Davies, Kane, Son (Lamela 71)

Unused subs: Gazzaniga, Wanyama, Llorente, Lucas Moura

Attendance: 66,099

....

In the event, another composed performance saw Spurs not only shut out Dortmund's formidable attack but in so doing prompt a good-natured beer-throwing celebration in the away end. Those standing on the vast terrace thought they were caught in a freak beer storm. Now, about that drinking in view of the pitch rule…

12

Tottenham Hotspur v Manchester City, 9 April 2019

SINCE OVERCOMING Dortmund, Spurs had continued to falter in the Premier League, losing to Southampton and Liverpool to end any lingering hopes of the title. Drawing Manchester City in the Champions League quarter-finals hardly lifted spirits but a momentous event soon did. The new stadium was finally open.

Fans had the first chance to enjoy the unique experience on 3 April for an evening Premier League game against Crystal Palace. They were absolutely blown away, as were Palace who succumbed to goals from Son Heung-min – a man on a mission to prove Spurs were not a one-man show as far as goalscoring was concerned

– and Christian Eriksen. Under the lights, fans could dream that a new era of glory nights was conceivable. In fact, that joyous evening was a small inkling of what was to come.

A week later, with just over 60,000 packed inside the stadium, Spurs and City walked out to the backdrop of a *tifo* display – fans holding aloft coloured bags spelling out To Dare Is To Do, the club motto, across the magnificent single tier South Stand – an image that has since provided the wallpaper for thousands of phones and computer screens.

Driven by the atmosphere, both teams went at each other and there was drama aplenty: a penalty, a goal, brinkmanship, pandemonium.

Son seizes the initiative but injury to Kane rocks Spurs

Sam Wallace, *Daily Telegraph*,
Tottenham Hotspur Stadium

It is all happening very fast at Tottenham Hotspur, who opened their first new stadium in 120 years last week and by next Wednesday could find themselves in the semi-finals of the European Cup for only the second time in a history that has rarely been as remarkable as this.

The second leg of this compelling Champions League quarter-final is some cliffhanger for the nation to wait a week for but, given the intensity of the first part, it will be quite a game at the Etihad Stadium.

Without Harry Kane, injured in the second half, a masterful finish from Son Heung-min with 12 minutes to play meant that Spurs are the team on top.

As a game it had a lot to take in, including the injury to Spurs' star player, in a collision with Fabian Delph that was largely of Kane's own making. Before that there was a video assistant referee review that led to a first-half penalty that few but Uefa would deem sensible, and then Sergio Agüero's subsequent miss.

The two sides played the game like it was a final, with plenty of energy and no little bad feeling – and the great noise in the new stadium at White Hart Lane was a response to that.

Afterwards, Mauricio Pochettino, the Spurs manager, gravely delivered the news that he believed it was possible Kane might not play again this season. It is the time of the season when the demands of the game take their toll, and do not discriminate between the great and the good. A Champions League semi-final without Kane would not be the same for Spurs, and in the first half in particular he looked the man for the occasion.

It was one of those nights when Pep Guardiola grimly defended his City players, even when it is plain they did not hit the standards we have come to expect.

They had more of the ball, but in the moments that really decide these emotionally charged occasions – that Agüero penalty especially – their nerve seemed to fail.

Guardiola left out Kevin De Bruyne and Leroy Sané and then brought them on for the final few minutes, when those in their place had not managed to dominate the game.

The City manager said he had decided to leave out De Bruyne in order to play two holding midfielders, Ilkay Gündogan and Fernandinho. He implied the Belgian would be back for the second leg, although last season there would have been no question of leaving him out of a tie like this, home or away.

As he looked ahead to that second leg, Guardiola dismissed the notion that this Spurs side were, as he once suggested, dependent on Kane and ran through their many options to play without their leading man.

On this night they did have some other heroes, although whether they will be enough to win Spurs the tie is another matter.

In midfield Harry Winks, back after a month away, and Moussa Sissoko were both excellent, and together they combined to give Spurs the edge. Riyad Mahrez, playing instead of Sané, was less decisive. These are the small margins, and towards the end of an exhausting season both managers expressed nothing less than gratitude for the effort of their players.

Spurs went at their visitors in the way few do when faced with Guardiola's team. They committed numbers forward and pressed their opposition. They looked like a side who had six days to prepare for this game. The full-backs, Danny Rose and Kieran Trippier, were high up the pitch and there was pressure on City every time Ederson looked to pass it out.

Nevertheless, no matter the number of white shirts swarming around them, City continued to play it out from the back. Guardiola refused to accept his players were showing the signs of fatigue, although he later hinted at the frustrations of such a compressed preparation time. He knows that, at this stage of the season, he cannot introduce a hint of doubt.

As for the penalty, both sets of players had looked satisfied with the award of a corner after 12 minutes when Danny Makkelie, the VAR, told referee Bjorn Kuipers he should take a look at the video screen. Rose had thrown himself down to his right to block Raheem Sterling's shot and the motion of his body meant that his left arm had been thrown into the air.

There had been contact with the ball somewhere on his arm, but he was so close when the shot was struck that it had barely registered among the players.

It requires a very single-minded referee to ignore the verdict of his VAR colleague that he has made a clear and obvious error. Under the current Uefa view, a case could be made for awarding the penalty.

The action of Rose's arm had made his body bigger, as Uefa see it. As a decision taking into account all the imperfections of the game as we know them, it was rotten.

Hugo Lloris saved Agüero's penalty to his left quite comfortably and the home support roared its approval. Spurs tried to force the issue after that, with Kane leading the way. He drew fouls from Nicolas Otamendi and then Fernandinho, a tangle on the pitch that looked more interesting than VAR seemed to have noticed.

The Brazilian appeared to have an elbow on top of the Englishman's head as they fell in a heap.

The incident that led to Kane's injury was a ball down the line from Delph, the stand-in left-back once more. It was the kind of tackle that often leads to the full-back being injured, when the challenge comes across and the man striking the ball kicks the hard sole of a boot. This one was different, with Kane's left ankle sliding underneath Delph's boot and the joint being forced into an unnatural bend on the turf.

Spurs had created more in the first half, with chances for Kane and Dele Alli, who was lively. After the break, they were pushed back by City, but then came Son.

Played in by Christian Eriksen down the right channel, he delayed his run to stay onside. When his first touch did not take him towards goal, he retrieved the ball on the touchline, doubled back past Ederson and then Delph and unleashed a shot with his left foot that beat the City goalkeeper on his line.

The Spurs team who finished the game, with Fernando Llorente on for Alli, who looked to have injured an arm, as well as Lucas Moura and Victor Wanyama, was a long way from first choice.

But this is the time of the season when the big games have to be won, whichever way they can.

....

Tottenham Hotspur 1   Manchester City 0
Son (78)

Tottenham Hotspur: Lloris, Trippier, Alderweireld, Vertonghen, Rose, Sissoko, Winks (Wanyama 81), Eriksen, Alli (Llorente 87), Son Heung-min, Kane (Lucas Moura 58)

Unused subs: Gazzaniga, Foyth, D Sánchez, Davies

Manchester City: Ederson, Walker, Otamendi, Laporte, Delph, Fernandinho, Gündogan, Mahrez (Sané 89), Silva (De Bruyne 89), Sterling, Agüero (Gabriel Jesus 71)

Unused subs: Kompany, Stones, Foden, Muric

Attendance: 60,044

....

From the beginning, the noise inside the stadium was the loudest many could recall hearing at a football match – prompting those who knew their history to remember the tales of the wall of sound in the famous semi-final game against Benfica in 1962. At the start of proceedings, the crowd was so loud that the Champions League music, which commercial reality dictates must be played at top volume just in case the people at the game make their presence felt a little too much, was drowned out. Emotions were roused further 12 minutes into the game when City were contentiously awarded a penalty. Sergio Agüero stepped up but, possibly unnerved by the noise from the South Stand behind the goal he was shooting at, saw his weak attempt saved by Lloris.

At the end of the game large sections of the support decamped to the stadium bars, which were still full well after the final whistle. And those on Tottenham High Road hosted impromptu parties well into Wednesday morning. Some were starting to believe.

13

Manchester City v Tottenham Hotspur, 17 April 2019

A TRIP to Manchester for a European tie brought back memories of the anti-climax of having to play a European final in Wolverhampton back in 1972. It wasn't supposed to happen this way.

All the same, Spurs fans travelled in numbers to the Etihad Stadium on an uncharacteristically warm spring day, trying to be positive without truly believing.

Spurs had continued to stumble in the league, taking just seven points from the last 21 available, with no guarantee of a fourth place and Champions League football once again. Moreover, the North West was not a happy hunting ground; and City were City and arguably the best team in Europe.

VAR gives Spurs victory in game for all seasons

Henry Winter, *The Times*, Etihad Stadium

One of the maddest, most memorable games in Champions League history ended with Tottenham Hotspur drawing on all their reserves of resilience, and an unlikely decisive reserve in Fernando Llorente, to reach the semi-finals. Spurs had to survive a late scare when VAR rescued them, ruling out a Raheem Sterling goal for a Sergio Agüero offside, ending Manchester City's hopes of the quadruple.

The only frustrations for Spurs was the groin injury suffered by Moussa Sissoko and the booking for the outstanding Son Heung-min which rules him out of the first leg of the semi-final against Ajax. Yet such was the quality of the football that both sides were applauded off at the end.

This was football from the playground, joyous, breathless, relentlessly positive, the type of matches that become celebrated in T-shirts and video bestsellers. This was football the way it should be played, upbeat, we attack, you attack, pure entertainment. This was football that makes children fall in love with the game, with the excitement, the chance of self-expression. The intensity demanded by Pep Guardiola was instantly there, a crackling atmosphere whipped up by the City fans, and a sense of urgency brimming in all of his players. Spurs responded, playing the Mauricio Pochettino front-foot way, the Spurs' 'to dare is to do' way.

All present, and the millions tuning in, were treated to something very special. The prize was a semi-final against Ajax, and maybe the irrepressible football of the young Dutch princes stirred the imagination of City and Spurs even more.

No game in Champions League history had witnessed such a frenetic, free-scoring opening, the fastest four goals ever in Europe's elite competition. They arrived within 12 minutes, then a fallow period of ten minutes until the fifth. Accusing fingers can be pointed at some of the defending, but the quality of the attacking needs celebrating.

Both sides contributed handsomely, going for it time after time. Son was immense for Spurs, his movement constantly catching City's defence out. Lucas Moura's pace exploited the hosts' high line. Dele Alli drifted around, collecting possession, turning and looking for team-mates.

But City had so much class and character. Hunger ran through them. Kevin De Bruyne brought such guile and urgency to midfield. One of his turns was so sudden that Sissoko damaged his right adductor trying to keep close, and limped away, too slowly for Cüneyt Çakır, the Turkish referee who booked him.

Bernardo Silva's delivery was constantly measured, picking out friendly feet, whatever the pressure Spurs tried to place on him. Agüero was creating and scoring, the model centre-forward with his touch, movement and constant desire for the ball.

The glittering gem for City was Sterling, magnificent in that astonishing first half of the first half, taking his tally for the season for club and country to 29 goals in 50 appearances. Deployed on the left, with Bernardo right, Sterling gave Kieran Trippier, his England team-mate, a torrid time with his movement, quick and clever, and his finishing, right foot, left foot, lethal. With voting continuing for footballer of the year, Sterling presented even more evidence as to why he is Virgil van Dijk's main rival for the honour. His finishing has been so enhanced working under Guardiola and Mikel Arteta, as well as determination to practise in pursuit of perfection.

Sterling began the goal rush after four minutes, biding his time on the left before making his telling run. The ubiquitous De Bruyne began the move on the right, passing into Agüero, taking the return and then laying the ball left to Sterling. City's No 7 now has ice in his veins at such moments, focusing only on the optimum way to damage the opponent.

He's quick but not hurried, controlling the situation. Taming De Bruyne's pass with the outside of his right foot, Sterling nudged the ball forward before his right foot began the night's festival of finishing. Trippier stood off, his eyes betraying only alarm. Toby Alderweireld shrunk from the scene as Sterling curled the ball around him and beyond the reach of the diving Hugo Lloris: 1-0.

Spurs responded superbly, equalising within three minutes and then taking the lead three minutes on. Son's first came when Sissoko found Christian Eriksen, Moura turned away from De Bruyne before passing in to Alli. Aymeric Laporte's attempted clearance simply teed up Son, whose first-time strike was straight at Ederson but the Brazilian was diving to his right, deceived by Spurs' intentions, and the ball slipped through his legs and in: 1-1.

Laporte has been such a reliable defensive presence for City this season, arguably their best defender, yet his touch let him down again here when trying to control Bernardo's crossfield pass. Moura nicked the ball, raced away from Ilkay Gündogan before checking back. Eriksen took over, stroking the ball across to Son, who took a touch before curling his shot beyond the outstretched left hand of Ederson: 1-2.

City were level within a minute, punishing Spurs as they were still intoxicated by taking the lead. City went for them, David Silva and Agüero working the ball across to Bernardo, whose shot clipped Danny Rose's right leg and flew in past Lloris: 2-2.

Spurs tried to calm things down. Lloris took time over his goalkicks. But City restored their lead after 21 minutes, and again it was through Sterling's nerveless finishing, slamming the ball in with his left foot from a tight angle from De Bruyne's marvellous cross: 3-2.

Trippier and Eriksen threw their arms up in frustration. This was such a huge chance to reach the semi-finals. They were missing the talismanic Harry Kane but Son was in such deadly mood. When Sissoko finally hobbled away four minutes from the break, it seemed an overly adventurous decision by Pochettino to replace a holding midfield player with a centre forward. Llorente went up front, Son went right, and the momentum accelerated in City's favour.

They dominated the start of the second half, Lloris saving from Sterling and then De Bruyne, rescuing Spurs. But just before the hour, De Bruyne slid the ball from left to right to Agüero, whose finish thundered past Lloris: 4-2.

So now it was City going through to face Ajax. But Spurs refused to go quietly as this incredible game continued to take the breath away. After 73 minutes, Trippier lifted in a corner that cleared Vincent Kompany and hit the jumping Llorente on the arm, and then hip and diverted past Ederson. The decision went to VAR, and Cakir jogged across to the screen with hundreds of nearby City fans offering advice. After careful consideration, the experienced Turkish official decided it was accidental, and awarded the goal: 4-3.

Pochettino tried to close the game down, sending on Ben Davies for Moura with Rose stepping up on to the left side of midfield. Spurs were now 4-1-4-1 with Victor Wanyama anchoring and Llorente leading the line. With the clock running down, and the quadruple on the line, Guardiola withdrew a full back for a winger,

Benjamin Mendy for Leroy Sané. Pochettino made his final change, taking off the tiring Rose and inserting Davinson Sánchez into defence.

Guardiola resembled a man on the edge of a nervous breakdown, leaping up and down and then holding his head in his hands in disbelief when Sterling's rapturously-received goal was ruled out for an Agüero offside.

© The Times/News Licensing

....

Manchester City 4   **Tottenham Hotspur 3**

Sterling (4, 21),   Son Heung-min (7, 10),
Bernardo Silva (11), Agüero (59) Llorente (73)

Manchester City: Ederson, Walker, Kompany, Laporte, Mendy (Sané 84), De Bruyne, Gündogan, Silva (Fernandinho 63), Bernardo Silva, Agüero, Sterling

Unused subs: Stones, Muric, Mahrez, Otamendi, Gabriel Jesus

Tottenham Hotspur: Lloris, Trippier, Alderweireld, Vertonghen, Rose (D Sánchez 90+1), Wanyama, Sissoko (Llorente 41), Alli, Eriksen, Lucas Moura (Davies 82), Son

Unused subs: Gazzaniga, Walker-Peters, Foyth, Skipp

Attendance: 53,348

....

Oh what a night. What transpired was an unforgettable evening, one of the great European games of all time.

Too often, supporting football is compared to a rollercoaster ride. On this occasion, that would be an understatement. One moment at the end summed it up. One fan turned to another and said: 'I think we've got this.' Sterling scored. 'Why did you say that?' screamed the second fan in frustration. Then VAR intervened. And both descended into the mass of flailing limbs that engulfed the away section.

Bernie Kingsley, a stalwart member of Spurs supporters' associations, tells of watching with friends in the City end. 'It gave a fascinating perspective, especially for that final disallowed goal,' he said. 'They were going mental with joy when it went in, I was going mental at Eriksen for giving the ball away and not surprisingly being ignored. Then the VAR thing went up on the screen and time stood still, followed by delirium at the Spurs end of the stadium and stunned silence and disbelief all around me. I had the biggest grin as I quietly fist-pumped. Surreal.'

An exuberant, mind-boggling contest spawned, in the weeks to come, a terrace anthem described by Spurs blogger Alan Fisher as 'unlike any Spurs chant I can recall, less a football chant, more a piece of storytelling and mythmaking. Perhaps also the first football song to celebrate VAR.' Frowned upon by some because it appropriated a chant adopted by Liverpool fans, who had themselves taken and adapted a chant based on a 1980s Italian disco classic (*L'Estate Sta Finedo* – or *The Summer Is Ending* – since you're asking) sung by fans in Italy, Spain, Portugal and, er, Scotland, it was nonetheless embraced with gusto by Spurs fans, gestating in the febrile atmosphere of the new stadium's South Stand goal line bar.

> *City thought they'd won it, but Tottenham*
>   *pulled it back,*
> *Wanyama in the middle, Llorente in attack,*
> *Sterling scored the winner, the Etihad went mad,*
> *The ref went to the camera, and it was disallowed*
> *Allez, Allez, Allez*

It was a good night for Eurostar, too, as many an Amsterdam trip was booked in the early hours of that morning.

14

Tottenham Hotspur v Ajax, 30 April 2019

THREE DAYS before the Dutch visitors were due to arrive, Spurs succumbed at home to West Ham to end any hopes that the new ground may become a fortress. It was the familiar, if frustrating, story of late; the team not being smart enough, or sharp enough, to break down their obdurate opponents.

Ajax arrived as the surprise package of the competition; a skilful, confident, young, energetic team which in despatching both Real Madrid and Juventus had attracted much praise and adulation, inviting comparison with their pioneering predecessors of the 1970s. Before the game, the notion that both sets of fans had an affinity took a knock when skirmishes and masonry throwing were witnessed on the High Road. Ajax had travelled in numbers, their Ultras taking over central London's Leicester Square for hours leading up to the game.

Ahead of kick-off, the South Stand once again displayed the now familiar *tifo* – To Dare Is To Do – and the wall of sound was in full flow in the opening stages, collectively pinching itself at witnessing a Champions League semi-final so soon in Spurs' sparkling new home.

Donny van de Beek leaves sluggish Spurs on the brink in Champions League

> Miguel Delaney, *The Independent*,
> Tottenham Hotspur Stadium

An exacting performance from Europe's most exciting young team, against a Tottenham Hotspur that are going to have to do so much more to keep this Champions League dream alive.

Sure, this 1-0 win wasn't the complete football exhibition it initially promised to be from Ajax, but was an exhibition of other qualities. As Spurs tried to bludgeon them after Donny van de Beek's brilliant early goal, they showed their mature resolve, and a resilience.

That doesn't bode well for Spurs' attempts to overturn this semi-final in the second leg, but they will at least have Son Heung-min back, if not Jan Vertonghen. The defender's head injury will prompt a lot of questions about how he was allowed back onto the pitch before looking like he was going to collapse but, as regards the play, the change it necessitated did prompt a recovery from Spurs that at least prevented Ajax pretty much securing a place in the Madrid final in this first leg.

The first half-hour was one of those exhibitions that you sense will come to be seen as a signature spell for a team, one of those periods of play permanently looked back on. Ajax were that good; that dominant.

Tottenham haven't been given a chasing like this in a long time, by any team, in any stadium. Few stadiums in Europe – in truth – will have witnessed such moments of realisation like this, that this is no surprise underdog. Ajax looked as good as pretty much any prestige side over the last decade.

The excellence of the technical execution was good enough, but to combine it with such fluency of movement was so often spectacular.

That was conducted by the brilliant Frenkie De Jong, with everything stemming from his sense of control. He decided when to up it, when to slow it, when to cut through, when to open out.

The goal was such a natural follow-on from this, as well as the outlet provided by the clever running of attackers like van de Beek.

From that wider player, Ajax's control and movement in tight spaces is then just exquisite. So it was that Hakim Ziyech slipped van de Beek in, for the midfielder to hit another angled finish.

The Spurs defence did seem to stop at that moment, apparently thinking it was offside. That was checked by referee Alberto Undiano Mallenco and given, but wasn't the only time the home backline needed to take a moment.

It also emphasised it wasn't all Ajax.

Pochettino already had a tactical dilemma without the outlets of Harry Kane and Son Heung-min up front, or the direction of Harry Winks in the middle, but the decision to go with three at the back against a false nine in Dusan Tadic seemed to further play into Ajax's feet and just open up more space for them. The three centre-halves just didn't know where to go.

It was why the obviously more important real-life problem of Vertonghen's injury did bring an in-game solution for Pochettino. It forced him to go to his most experienced player on the bench, in Moussa Sissoko, and also to four in the middle.

It was very quickly a different game. Spurs had cut off Ajax's channels of attack, and were now picking up steam themselves, if mostly through the running of Lucas Moura.

Their pressure was nowhere near as aesthetically pleasing as the Dutch side's, but it was just as effective. The game became about physicality against finesse.

Spurs were now hoping to bludgeon Ajax back, but it only brought forth a different set of qualities from a young side: impressive resolve.

They held their ground with less possession, and instead looked to try and pick Spurs off when they could. One such moment almost led to what would surely have been the clinching goal, as Tadic fed David Neres to hit the inside of the post.

They didn't get that second goal, but did get a remarkable third successive away win in the Champions League knock-outs.

That is hugely impressive. That is the team Spurs must overcome.

© The Independent

Tottenham Hotspur 0   **Ajax 1**

van de Beek (15)

Tottenham Hotspur: Lloris, Alderweireld, D Sánchez, Vertonghen (Sissoko 39), Trippier (Foyth 80), Wanyama, Eriksen, Alli, Rose (Davies 79), Llorente, Lucas Moura

Unused subs: Gazzaniga, Walker-Peters, Dier, Skipp

Ajax: Onana, Veltman, de Ligt, Blind, Tagliafico, Schöne (Mazraoui 65), de Jong, Ziyech (Huntelaar 87), van de Beek, Neres, Tadic

Unused subs: Sinkgraven, Magallán, Dolberg, Semedo Varela, de Wit

Attendance: 60,243

Ajax brought their own brand of atmosphere to a ground still finding its feet, and their support on the night was as infectious as the football their team played. But once again it appeared that the seeming obsession with losing semi-finals would round off another frustrating season. Attempting to make the best of it, one fan was heard recounting a dream in which Spurs were 4-0 up in the final minute of the Champions League final but then 'Trump presses the button' he said, before pausing to add with a grin, 'Why do these things always happen to us?' All the same, those Eurostar tickets weren't going to waste.

15

Ajax v Tottenham Hotspur, 8 May 2019

THE BIGGEST game in decades and Amsterdam's myriad attractions made it certain that thousands more Spurs fans would travel than had tickets, many opting to spend a few spring days in the town as well as take in the game.

Despite some nervousness from the police beforehand, it all passed off pleasantly enough. Spurs fans flooded the town, and the bars around Dam Square racked their prices up. More of that unique Champions League hospitality on display.

Packed in front of every available screen in every available bar, Spurs fans who arrived the night before the match watched amazing scenes unfold at Anfield as Liverpool staged a comeback few imagined possible to beat Messi's Barcelona and reach the final for the second year in a row. Totally unexpected, but any talk of whether it was worse to be beaten in the final by Liverpool or Barcelona was quickly silenced by a harsh dose of reality. Spurs had to get there first.

The Johan Cruyff Arena, as befits its name, is a wonderful stage for a grand football occasion. The away facilities are comparatively decent, the sightlines are good and the atmosphere is exhilarating. But by half-time the attraction for Spurs fans was wearing off. Their team were 2-0 down and seemingly heading inexorably for the exit. As the teams re-emerged, the home crowd tempted fate and began to sing the old Bob Marley hit *'Don't worry, about a thing, 'cos every little thing, gonna be alright.'*

Moura's hat-trick snatches dramatic victory

Henry Winter, *The Times*, Johan Cruyff Arena

When Lucas Moura drove the ball deep into the Ajax net deep into stoppage time for the third time, the home players slumped to the floor. This was an incredible finish, testament to Tottenham Hotspur's belief and resilience and the shooting of Moura. This was further proof of the brilliance of Champions League football.

Can we play this every week? This year's Champions League has become so much more than the greatest club competition of them all. It has turned into a celebration of character, of skilful, spirited football, of the game as art and heart. Tottenham gave everything here, and the Johan Cruyff Arena finally fell silent when Moura completed his hat-trick deep into stoppage time to set up an all-English final with Liverpool in Madrid.

Spurs have become used to confronting adversity this season, having recovered from gleaning only one point from their first three group-stage games, but this was extraordinary. They were being outplayed, but then Mauricio Pochettino sent on Fernando Llorente, and Moura made all the difference.

For 55 minutes, until Moura gave them hope with those two quick goals, Spurs were listless, laboured and utterly outclassed. Their second-half bravura display was such a contrast to their performance earlier. Dele Alli was involved, Kieran Trippier was storming down the right and Moura was wriggling into finishing positions.

Earlier, they were taught a lesson in the use of possession. It seemed until the second half that Spurs were not simply trying to stifle 11 talented footballers, they were taking on a movement. Ajax's philosophy is everywhere here, framed in pictures of Dennis Bergkamp and Marco van Basten on the walls, and in the very name itself, the Johan Cruyff Arena. VIPs heading towards the sleek escalators paused to have their photos taken by the bust of the late, great Cruyff. Outside, in the stands, Ajax supporters sang of Cruyff. Down on the field, the latest generation quickly showed again they have seized the mantle passed down from Ajax legends of yesteryear.

The philosophy lives on in the skill and movement of the all-purpose midfielder Frenkie de Jong, who was passing wide one moment, unerringly finding friendly feet, then nicking the ball off Son Heung-min the next moment, and then again. For students seeking the essence of Ajax's philosophy, De Jong ran a masterclass in Amsterdam for almost an hour. He looked intent on organising rolling rondos up the field, with Spurs spectating.

At one point, De Jong calmly joined forces with Lasse Schone and Daley Blind and worked the ball in triangles through bemused Spurs players and upfield, past Alli and Moura. On one venture into midfield, Victor Wanyama simply stood in his way, having lost all confidence in stopping the young Dutchman legally. Barcelona have recruited shrewdly in De Jong, who will stir some life into a midfield that shrunk so embarrassingly against Liverpool at Anfield on Tuesday evening.

De Jong was not the only young master at work. The latest disciples of this rarefied footballing religion included Donny van de Beek, Spurs' nemesis in the home leg, who was busy doing backheels to Hakim Ziyech, not for show, but because it was the swiftest way to manipulate the ball under pressure to his team-mate.

The next moment Van de Beek was stealthily dispossessing Moussa Sissoko, creating as well as destroying. Van de Beek put in one tackle, forceful but fair, on Wanyama that left the Kenyan crumpled on the pristine turf. Ajax can play, and look after themselves too.

Wanyama did not reappear after the break.

Ajax's creed of urging expression and responsibility-taking, whatever the age, was there immeasurably in their teenaged defensive colossus, Matthijs de Ligt, who made it 1-0 on the night, 2-0 on aggregate, after five minutes. Hugo Lloris repelled an Ajax attack, pushing away Dusan Tadic's shot at the expense of a corner, and De Ligt cashed in. Schone curled the corner across and Spurs fans in the corner must have been rubbing their eyes in disbelief at the lack of marking.

Trippier appeared charged with combating De Ligt, a fiery featherweight against a smooth, composed heavyweight, the mother of all mismatches. He didn't even have a ladder. Trippier did not stay with De Ligt's run long as the defender hurtled towards Schone's delivery and headed powerfully in.

And what of Spurs? For 55 minutes until Moura hinted at a remarkable recovery mission, they looked exhausted by the season, by the small squad, by the loss of players like Harry Kane. Son returned from suspension and tried to bring some energy to Spurs, and one run in from the left did lead to his hitting the post.

Alli tried some flicks, as usual, and launched one briefly promising attack with Danny Rose, but really came to life only after the interval. Christian Eriksen, teed up by Moura, did manage a shot but little fazed André Onana until the second half.

Ajax supporters delighted in the joy and mastery of their football, and the ease with which Premier League visitors were being swept aside. 'You're shit and you know you are,' they sang in English so crisp you could almost feel the apostrophe.

Their delight grew further nine minutes from the interval when Trippier endured another moment to forget, when Spurs folded again. Tadic began the move, being too fast for Trippier, and Van de Beek took over, pushing on, those famous shirts flocking forward. Tadic then took over, and his pass to Ziyech opened Spurs up. Every pass had value, precision and thought. Ziyech gave Lloris no chance with a strong finish.

But there is a resilience to Pochettino's side, and the introduction of Llorente in attack gave them more of a focus. Eriksen found Alli, whose effort was saved by Onana, and suddenly the memory of Ajax's first-half control faded. Spurs believed.

Ten minutes into the new half, the new dawn, Alli raced through the middle, finally eluding De Jong, and slipping the ball to Moura. He cut inside and sent a low shot past Onana. 'Come on you Spurs' cut through the incessant Dutch chants. Four minutes later, Spurs truly believed. Son was finding space now, and slipped the ball down the right for the overlapping Trippier, at last resembling the marauding force of last year. His ball was met by Llorente, but Onana saved. The ball squirmed to Moura, who was too quick for De Ligt and stroked the ball in from a tight angle.

Ajax fans were betraying few nerves, constantly urging their team on, and they almost scored with 12 minutes remaining when Ziyech, released by De Jong, hit a post.

But Spurs immediately returned to hammering at Ajax's door. Eriksen lifted in another cross, and Llorente caused chaos in the area, the ball popping up to Jan Vertonghen, whose header bounced back off the bar.

Spurs were so committed to attack and Ajax almost scored on the counter but Toby Alderweireld slid across to deny De Jong.

The Dutch fans kept singing. Yet Spurs kept believing, kept pushing for the goal that would take them to the final. Lloris even came up for a late corner. But then Llorente and Alli combined, and Moura scored. The final should be a classic.

....

Ajax 2
de Ligt (5), Ziyech (35)

Tottenham Hotspur 3
Lucas Moura (55, 59, 90+6)

Ajax: Onana, Mazraoui, de Ligt, Blind, Tagliafico, Schöne (Veltman 60), de Jong, Ziyech, van de Beek (Magallán, 90), Neres, Dolberg (Sinkgraven 67)

Unused subs: Huntelaar, Traore, Semedo Varela, de Wit

Tottenham Hotspur: Lloris, Trippier (Lamela 81), Alderweireld, Vertonghen, Rose (Davies 82), Sissoko, Wanyama (Llorente 45), Eriksen, Alli, Son, Lucas Moura

Unused subs: Gazzaniga, Dier, Foyth, Skipp

Attendance: 52,641

For Spurs fans in the away section it will be hard to erase the memory of the minutes as the clock ticked down and the resulting hour-long holdback in the ground as the favourite from any trip undertaken anywhere. The split second of disbelief followed swiftly by utter pandemonium as Lucas Moura's winner went in, fans and revelling stewards hugging and grinning, Poch sunk to his knees, the Ajax players prostrate on the ground, the Spurs staff and squad with Poch running to celebrate with the fans in front of the away corner, the call and response celebration with every player, the bonding of playing and coaching staff and fans in one big, tears-of joy, let-it-all-out love in. It's impossible to recall the scene without the emotion coming back in waves.

Long-time fan, blogger and author Alan Fisher captured what the moment meant to fans, as he so often does. 'There is nothing, nothing ever like Moura's winner at Ajax. This is stuff beyond dreams, one of the greatest ever moments of unadulterated joy. This is the stuff of miracles and wonder, in an age when it's supposedly all entitlement and money. This is about discovering childhood again, when all things are possible, discovering why we fell in love with the club and the game. Don't worry about exaggerating what it was like – you can't.'

Poch knew what it meant too. Through tears of joy he said: 'Thank you, football, thank you, these guys, my players... they are heroes. In the last year, I am telling everyone that I have a group of players who are heroes. Second half was amazing. Thank you, thank you, football. This type of emotion, without football, it is impossible to live. Thank you for the people that believe.' Not half, gaffer.

Five times Spurs had come back from the brink of extinction. Two sensational nights away from home had not only restored the glory but given it a new sheen in the most undreamt, implausible fashion, not just for Spurs and their supporters, but for the watching football world. Some football experiences are so wondrous, they belong to all of us.

Commentating on BT Sport, Darren Fletcher delivered one of the great snippets of commentary, one that will resonate with Spurs fans the way 'They think it's all over' does for England fans.

'Ben Davies with the tackle… Here's Son… Sissoko… Here's Dele Alli… Here's Lucas Moura… Oh they've done it! I cannot believe it! With the last kick of the game! Tottenham Hotspur are heading to the Champions League final!'

It wasn't all over. Spurs were going to Madrid.

The father of push and run, Spurs manager Arthur Rowe, talks to his players at White Hart Lane in 1950

The team of the century, Bill Nicholson's super Spurs, with the Double trophies in 1961

A touch of humour from the fans establishes a legend in 1962 as Spurs face Benfica in the European Cup semi-final

Bill Nick walks Jimmy Greaves into White Hart Lane after signing him from AC Milan for a British record £99,999 in 1962

Alan Mullery leaves the pitch through a crowd of fans and police, clutching the UEFA Cup after Spurs beat Wolves on home ground in 1972

Keith Burkinshaw (centre) parades World Cup winners Ricky Villa (left) and Ossie Ardiles to an astonished audience in 1978

Glenn Hoddle, for many fans the most skilful and creative player ever to grace the turf at White Hart Lane, in action in 1984

Spurs celebrate the 1984 UEFA Cup win over Anderlecht at White Hart Lane, the second European trophy won in N17

Superstar Jürgen Klinsmann arrives at Tottenham Hotspur's training ground in 1994

Manager Martin Jol, who brought the good times back to Spurs, applauds the fans in 2006

Gareth Bale terrorising the Internazionale defence again on an unforgettable night in North London in 2010

Mauricio Pochettino with coaching colleagues Miguel D'Agostino, Jésus Perez and Toni Jiménez signs for Daniel Levy in May 2016

Harry Kane and Poch – you can't have one without the other

Barcelona's Lionel Messi leads Spurs a dance in the Champions League at Wembley, September 2018

Wembley rises as the great Dane Christian Eriksen puts Spurs ahead against Internazionale, November 2018

Lucas Moura sends Spurs through at the last against Barcelona at the Nou Camp, December 2018

The first European night at the new Tottenham Hotspur stadium, with Manchester City the opponents, April 2019

Fernando Llorente celebrates Spurs' third goal in a cracking quarter-final second leg at the Etihad Stadium, April 2019

Emotional scenes at the Johan Cruyff Arena in Amsterdam after Spurs reach the Champions League Final, May 2019

The Spurs end in the Champions League Final at the Wanda Metropolitano Stadium in Madrid, June 2019

16

Tottenham Hotspur v Liverpool, 1 June 2019

THERE WERE three weeks between the victory over Ajax and the final, three weeks that were a time of suspended delight. The last league game of the season became a sideshow as fans in the new stadium partied and sang of Madrid, of that extraordinary night in Manchester, and of Lucas Moura in Amsterdam.

A team that had made no signings for two transfer windows, that had no home venue for most of the season, and that had teetered on the brink of elimination not once or twice but six times, was going to play in the biggest club game in the world – so unexpected yet so hoped for. Supporters could not help but savour the excitement and to think of what victory would mean. It would end the argument once and for all about whether the club belonged among the elite. Only 22 clubs had lifted the trophy since its inception. Only five had won all three European club trophies. Make no mistake, winning would dramatically change the club and its standing in the eyes of the entire football world, Arsenal fans included.

Simply being there changed everything, too. Spurs were global headline news. Fans could bask in the attention and the glory. But the harsh realities didn't take long to kick in. Demand for tickets was off the scale, and yet only 16,616 would be available to Spurs, half of the 52% allocated to the finalists. Of course, many of the remaining 48% would find their way to fans via a black market that would see asking prices reach a staggering £16,000 a ticket.

Getting to Madrid was also a challenge. Having qualified 24 hours after Liverpool, Spurs fans found that the price and availability of flights and hotel rooms was already skewed by the enormous demand from the Reds' fans. Getting a flight direct from the UK to Madrid was virtually impossible by the morning after that unforgettable night before in Amsterdam. Elaborate routes were researched, elaborate plans for securing accommodation hatched.

One fan who made it to Madrid, a former Spurs season-ticket holder who had moved to Toronto but had wanted, like so many others who had no chance of a ticket, to be there for the occasion, gave an example of the huge international following both clubs have. Trying to book a flight direct to Madrid from Toronto the day after Spurs qualified, he found every seat booked. The story was repeated in cities across the globe.

An estimated 100,000 fans reached the Spanish capital for the weekend of 1 June. And despite predictably lurid headlines about 'English hooligans' in the Spanish tabloids, there was not a hint of trouble. Fans mixed and partied and enjoyed the sun. The Spanish authorities laid on two huge fan parks for the afternoon of the game, but closed them before kick-off, leaving those fans without tickets to find a bar with a TV screen with, inevitably, prices to match those charged by UEFA to the fans, of whom they make great play of saying the game is all about. UEFA's positioning as the omnipotent brand in the football universe they like to portray themselves as – 'we care about football' – has a hollow ring to it.

Rumour has it that even the boards of the two clubs from England's mega-monied Premier League raised eyebrows at the prices charged for the final. While the cheapest tickets were £60, not unreasonable for a game of this magnitude, 54% of the tickets were priced at £154, a further 21% at £385, and 5% at an astonishing £513. Those who secured tickets in those price bands in seats with restricted views could pay the bargain price of £120, £308 or £410 respectively. That's £410 to not see the game properly.

Thomas Cook Sport, which provided travel options for fans of both clubs, crumbled under the unprecedented pressure on one of the busiest days in UK airport history. Some fans who had booked day trips were still in the UK on the afternoon of the game; one plane, delayed by a bird strike on its engine, got its passengers to Madrid but, despite a police escort rushing them to the stadium, they missed the first ten minutes of the biggest game of their lives.

For others who made the game on time, there was more evidence of the reality for fans that lies behind the marketing gloss. Signposting from the station Spurs fans were recommended to use was non-existent, as were the water stations promised to help them on the 25-minute walk to the stadium in 35-degree heat. Once there, fans milled around to find their entrances, again inadequately signposted, as prowling police exuded low-level hostility.

Some witnessed random police attacks on individual fans; others saw 'stewards' dressed in yellow tabards asking to check tickets before running off with them, fans left to point out the scam and warn other fans as the police and official stewards looked on. Inside the designated fanzone on the stadium perimeter they found long queues, no shelter from the baking sun, and steep prices.

But this was a Champions League Final and the ordeals of getting there only served to make the sweet smell of success in being there that much more valued, if not entirely appreciated. Huddled in the few yards of shade by the stadium walls, singing the campaign songs and catching up with old friends, fans began to get videos through on their mobile phones of the scenes on Tottenham High Road. It had apparently been packed since midday, the roads closed off three hours before the match as 62,000 arrived to watch the game in the new stadium on giant TV screens, and thousands more populated the bars and cafes and pavements outside. The clips showed fans packing the street as far as the lens could pan. As the singing from the stadium in London was heard over mobile phones, the crowds at the stadium in Madrid responded, a call and response for the digital age.

Once inside, there was a pause to take in the unfamiliar glory of it all. The sheer numbers and the flags that festooned every available wall and balcony, the strangeness of playing a familiar English opponent in a foreign city.

The story of a game that ultimately failed to live up to those hoping for a football feast, and certainly those expecting the most glorious Spurs glory night yet, is told by Miguel Delaney below.

Liverpool's European victory was years in the making

Miguel Delaney, *The Independent*, Wanda Metropolitano Madrid

Liverpool and Jürgen Klopp, finally, and doggedly, get there. They have won the first silverware of the German's era with the greatest club trophy of all and the sixth Champions League in this club's great history, to at last fulfil the potential of this team and this whole season, even if the performance in this 2-0 win over an even poorer Tottenham Hotspur did not reflect either. It was one of Liverpool's greatest recent moments, from one of the worst recent finals. That will not matter to a joyous Klopp or any of his players or supporters, much like with the ongoing debate over the initially decisive moment.

By the letter of the law, the ball striking the unfortunate Moussa Sissoko's arm was a penalty, allowing Mohamed Salah to score the key goal. That will be controversial but it was befitting of the season in its own way, given how many of these decisions there have been throughout this campaign, even if it did not in any way follow the raucous nature of so many of its matches – not least the semi-finals.

It was maybe just as well that Divock Origi's late strike ensured that a goal coming from a ball unluckily cannoning off a player's arm wasn't the only one in the game, but it did mean there was only ever going to be one winner.

It remains entirely debatable whether Spurs could have conjured a comeback had it stayed at 1-0 into stoppage time, whether they could have risen to it. They just couldn't rise to the occasion, although this was such a flat game. Whatever about fire-walking, it was often at walking pace.

Liverpool ultimately won it because they're just on a higher level, with more experience, more quality.

They didn't show it here at all, but they did show the necessary mettle.

To think the game opened with a moment that, well, should have opened it up. Except, rather than grab the occasion with both hands in the way Pochettino implored Tottenham Hotspur to, Sissoko stuck his hand out in a way that would have left his manager so frustrated. The ball eventually struck it and – by the rules in European competition – it was a penalty. With that decision coming after just 26 seconds, it would have been the quickest goal in Champions League final history, except for the wait. Whether that affected Salah we don't know, as his shot just about evaded Lloris.

That meant Paolo Maldini's goal from 2005 remained the quickest in history, but this was not the set-up for anything similar to Liverpool's last victory in the competition. It instead felt much more like a final from the 1970s to the 1990s, because it was so strangled by tension.

It was thereby impossible not to wonder whether the wait to actually play the game – let alone that before the penalty – had just made the players lose their rhythm, in the same way as the Europa League final first half.

Most of them just looked so rusty and off their game.

That was never better stated than with a number, as Opta revealed that this was at one point the Champions League with the lowest completion rate all season.

It must have been hard to count, as there were just so many examples. Spurs seemed guilty of the worst of them – Kieran Trippier in one first-half moment just playing the ball to nobody, Sissoko whacking out of play in another – and there was a sense that a certain anxiety at experiencing this stage for the first time was exacerbating their problems.

With Kane, however, there may have been something more. He just didn't look fully fit, having had to wait a lot longer than three weeks to play due to that injury in the quarter-final first leg against Manchester City.

It did not feel a coincidence that the move for the goal started with Virgil van Dijk completely bossing Kane and beating him to a loose ball, before it was played over the top for Mane.

Kane was admittedly a little more effective when he didn't have to move, such as with the clever touch that set up Spurs' best move of the first half. That released

Christian Eriksen, who then unleashed the best pass of the game through a brilliant through ball.

Reflecting so much of the match, though, Son Heung-min just couldn't take it on.

This was the problem with both sides. They were just lacking that focused intensity that so marks them out when they're at their best, making this one of the worst finals in some time.

Most of the opportunities – if that's what they can be described as – came from unintended bounces and deflections rather than any kind of concerted play. Every time something promising seemed to develop, there was a deflection or bad touch to divert it.

Spurs particularly needed that different energy, and it was little surprise that semi-final hero Lucas Moura was brought on. What might have been a surprise was who he was brought on for. It wasn't Kane but Harry Winks, who was another starting after a long injury absence. You just wouldn't have guessed it as much with him, as he had been one of the more competent players on the pitch. Spurs needed more than competence, though. They needed life.

They were all too quickly killed off. Origi was instead the substitute hero, not for the first time. He did ensure the final say. Liverpool got there in the end. It all had meaning, even if watching this match might have often caused people to doubt whether life had meaning.

That won't matter to Klopp or Liverpool. All that matters is that trophy.

....

Tottenham Hotspur 0   Liverpool 2

Salah (2, pen), Origi (87)

Tottenham Hotspur: Lloris, Trippier, Alderweireld, Vertonghen, Rose, Sissoko (Dier 74), Winks (Lucas Moura 66), Eriksen, Alli (Llorente 82), Son, Kane

Unused subs: Gazzaniga, Vorm, D Sánchez, Walker-Peters, Foyth, Aurier, Davies

Liverpool: Alisson, Alexander-Arnold, Matip, van Dijk, Robertson, Henderson, Fabinho, Wijnaldum (Milner 62), Salah, Firmino (Origi 58), Mané (Gomez 90)

Unused subs: Mignolet, Lovren, Sturridge, Moreno, Lallana, Oxlade-Chamberlain, Shaqiri, Brewster, Kelleher

Attendance: 63,272

....

The Spurs support gave a good account of itself, willing a lacklustre team on until Divock Origi's goal extinguished all hope. The trek back into the centre of Madrid was low-level chaos – the idea that football is for the fans is just a notion that the authorities pay lip-service to – with supporters in rueful but philosophical mood.

In the second half, Spurs had looked the better team, and most agreed that if they'd got a goal a tired-looking Liverpool would have crumbled. There was debate of course, about whether Kane or Lucas Moura should have started, but no real controversy at this stage. Such was the faith in Poch. And Kane. And of course, there was the penalty – a call very early on that utterly changed the game. Many thought, as Miguel Delaney did in his match report, that it was a penalty 'by the letter of the law' because they believed the new law on handball was in force for the game. But it wasn't, and what exactly the letter of the law that was in force should have led to was still being debated some six weeks after the final, including by the Premier League's head of refereeing.

The next day, sitting in a rooftop bar overlooking the splendour of central Madrid as the sun went down and the lights came up, a group of fans reflected on the events of a campaign none of them had imagined would lead them here. Had this been their team's one shot at glory? Was this as good as it got? Or was this the first taste of more to come? There was the overwhelming feeling that things had changed for good. Perchance to dream.

17

Marching on

MAGIC MOMENTS. Reality bites. Hopes and dreams. Improbable results. Business or pleasure. Football's fascination depends upon the push and pull of often conflicting emotions. Arthur Hopcraft, in his classic book *The Football Man*, observed that the game 'has conflict and beauty, and when those two qualities are present together in something offered for public appraisal they represent much of what I understand to be art.'

Conflict and beauty. A tension always present at the heart of the Spurs Way. Beauty certainly it was as the Lilywhites turned on the style way back in October 1960 when, as Ralph L Finn wrote in *The People*, 'Fabulous, fabulous Spurs. They were perfect, every man Jack of them. And I'm not being pretentious in awarding each of them maximum points [10 out of 10] in the Form Report. They strolled through the match like princes, taking an afternoon walk through their grounds. Though they slaughtered Nottingham Forest [4-0] that day they did it like gentlemen and were always as clean as they were clever'. Though never scaling those heights, there were spasmodic high-water marks through the years until comparable results arrived like a fleet of London buses in the Poch era: a 6-2 thumping of Everton at Goodison Park in December 2018 showed the team at its flowing, thrilling best. And there have been plenty of other examples – teaching Real Madrid a footballing lesson in November 2017; the back-to-back 6-1 and 7-1 romps over Leicester and Hull respectively in May 2017; the new year 2017 2-0 defeat of Chelsea at a delirious White Hart Lane; the 2-0 win over Manchester City in October 2016 that stripped away Pep Guardiola's air of infallibility; the pulsating 2-1 derby victory over Arsenal in February 2015 that signalled the start of a shift in power in North London.

Conflict when the glory is dimmed by the sharp perspective of results – the eternal debate about whether a fixation on style is drawing energy away from the necessity to win. The Spurs Way as a source of negative energy? Now that Poch's lemons are set out on his desk at the training ground to absorb bad vibes, is that conflict being resolved?

After the dust of a hot Madrid night has settled on Poch's fifth season in charge with Spurs agonisingly, frustratingly one step short of the ultimate glory, it is time to recognise that the club is at a turning point. Much has been achieved – so surprising yet so hoped for – but arguably the greatest challenge of all has still to be faced. With the state-of-the-art stadium and training facilities, the reputation as a Champions League club, a perennial Premier League contender, where do they go? The bar has been raised. What constitutes success is now driven by far more exacting criteria than ever before.

The constant refrain of 'Oh, but what has he won?' does Poch a disservice. It is a mistake to make winning a trophy the chief criterion when judging Poch's tenure. Spurs, don't forget, were never meant to be in a position where they were challenging for the title, reaching the Champions League Final, firmly establishing themselves in a Big Six – along with the two Manchester clubs, Liverpool, Chelsea and Arsenal – that appear to constitute a self-perpetuating league within the Premier

League. But always, looking down on the debate, is Danny Blanchflower, quizzically raising an eyebrow and reminding everyone: 'I said winning. With style.'

The dilemma resurfaced again in January 2019, when Spurs were knocked out of the League Cup, by Chelsea, and the FA Cup, by Crystal Palace, in the space of three days. At that stage the Premier League title was still in the balance, though the very idea that Spurs would go on to contest a Champions League Final would never have been contemplated. The domestic cups were seen as the most likely route to a trophy, and continual questions about Spurs' need to win a pot prompted a rare flash of annoyance from Poch. In the media conference after the Palace defeat, he made his feelings clear: 'Again we're going to have the debate whether a trophy will take the club to the next level. I don't agree with it. It only builds your ego. The most important thing for Tottenham right now is always to be in the top four.'

Maybe, but to dismiss the FA Cup touched a nerve with many fans. There's a special bond between Tottenham Hotspur and the FA Cup, or at least there is for the generation of fans who grew up when their club had won the trophy more times than any other, a generation who now formed a large section of the club's regular match-going support. And that's not to say that only fans of a certain age hold the FA Cup in high esteem – predilections are passed down through the years and the trophy features large in the collective psyche. Not to mention more than a few Chas 'n' Dave numbers. Although if Poch was a fan of the duo it's likely his mood following the Palace game may have been more accurately reflected by *There Ain't No Pleasing You* than *Hotshot Tottenham*.

That many have never witnessed their club win the trophy so central to its reputation rankles. So there was understandable consternation when the line-up for the FA Cup tie against Crystal Palace was known. Fans packed into the tight embrace of Selhurst Park's rudimentary away end asked themselves why they had bothered. Poch had picked an eleven that had not played together as a team before. And sure enough, that's how they performed. There was an all-pervading feeling of resentment that the best chance of a trophy had been wilfully thrown away because the manager thought the lure of the competition was one he could ignore.

Over the next few days Poch defended his stance in an attempt to try and get people to understand the scale of the challenge he faced. 'We [at] Tottenham [are] in a project that today is not only to win,' he said, going on to talk about the financial side, the stadium, the training facilities... a script well covered by his chairman for years. In fact, he referred directly to the plan Messrs Levy and Lewis had outlined to him from the outset. First, prepare the club to arrive in the new stadium – which presupposes a competitive, attractive team. Then, in the first season in the new home, create one that can finish in the top four the following season. So his team, it was implied, were way ahead of schedule.

And indeed they are. But the fixation with a top four place was unsettling. Not because Spurs supporters have ideas above their station – although what is fandom without aspiration? – but because their neighbours, who after borrowing Spurs' philosophy and taking it on to a higher plane, had reined in their ambition and were now deservedly drifting. What happens at Arsenal is always in the corner of the eye at Spurs, something that, vice versa, remains true despite Arsenal fans' protestations to the contrary. The veracity is underlined by the frequency with which it is deployed. The observation in the blue and white part of town, meanwhile, was that Arsenal may have qualified for the Champions League for 19 seasons in a row, but what was the point if they did nothing with it?

Comparisons with Arsenal also came thick and fast when the effect of the new Spurs stadium was considered, the perception being that the Gunners had begun to misfire because the cost of the Emirates had severely curtailed their ability to compete in the transfer market. In fact, Arsenal's project came in the midst of a very different economic cycle, and the club was able to capitalise on a very propitious property market to sell the site of its historic Highbury Stadium in well-heeled Islington, engage in property development and earn enormous profit. Arsenal last made a loss in 2002 and even after the stadium had opened had cash in reserve to the envy of the majority of other Premier League clubs. The interest payments on the stadium loans, though steep, were affordable. It suited the board and the manager, Arsène Wenger, to allow the perception that the club was strapped for cash because, like Poch, he preferred to acquire players he could mould, and thrived on the training pitch.

Daniel Levy had always tried to emphasise that the stadium finances were divorced from the football club finances. Transfer funds, he said on numerous occasions, were ring-fenced. But exactly how large was the ring? And would it have been much larger if there had been no stadium project?

What is known is that the club's main debt facility to finance the stadium is in the form of a £400m bullet, comparable to an interest-only mortgage, which matures in 2022 but is likely to be refinanced and perhaps even on better terms as the result of the increased revenue streams the club has attained. So during the lifetime of the debt only interest payments are made, estimated at around £50m per annum to service it. The cost of servicing the debt is amortised over a lengthy period, but of course provision must be made for repayment when the loan eventually matures. Spurs have seen their revenue expand exponentially since the move to Wembley and the opening of the new stadium; they banked £235m in broadcast income alone from the Premier League and UEFA in 2018/19. And that is pure profit, straight to the bottom line with no costs attached. The other key sources of income – commercial (sponsorship, advertising, merchandising and events), matchday (season ticket holders, box holders, corporate hospitality, through the gate, catering, and programmes) – have expanded interdependently along with the success of the team. And, hopefully, full potential is yet to be realised.

It may therefore come as no surprise, then, to hear that the club, under the prudent financial direction of Messrs Levy, Lewis and finance director Matthew Collecott, is unlikely to run into insurmountable difficulties over the stadium. However, the prerequisite of a successful business is a successful team. Having got themselves into the position they have never been in before – regular challengers for the Premier League and Champions League finalists – the definitions of what constitutes success for the team is narrowed. Spurs in 2019 cannot afford to finish outside the top four in the Premier League, or fail to reach the knockout stage in the Champions League, and must all the while deliver the brand of football they have won plaudits for, staying faithful to the brand they have become.

Talk of brands invariably irks football traditionalists, and it's easy to understand why. The commercialisation of the game has tried the patience of fans who have been exploited, their loyalty tested by high ticket prices and the cost of merchandising and TV subscriptions. Because fans are different from customers. A customer can take their business elsewhere, a fan can't. Loyal

M&S shoppers do not beat themselves up if they go to Waitrose from time to time to take advantage of their special offers. On the other hand, however miffed the denizens of the Lane were in the past by the poor fare on offer, they were never going to pitch up at Highbury or the Emirates. For them, football is not just any kind of football, it's Spurs football. Football fans are the most loyal of customers and football clubs the strongest of brands, providing both rational and emotional values and benefits and only limited by their partisanship.

So maybe the popular refrain of 'we are not customers, we are fans' is counterproductive. Successful clubs don't really have to push themselves to keep their audience content because they are great brands in themselves, and fans will always want to be associated with them and flock to them, attracted and retained not so much by elaborate promotional efforts but by the umbilical ties of family or community handed down from generation to generation. Why then should clubs try as hard as those businesses who have to attract customers to survive when they have fans aplenty? Yet if they only asked themselves 'what is it that we can do that the fans want?' and then use research to find out and guide them in their decision making, then maybe fans would be treated more like customers to be wooed and cherished.

The Spurs brand with its unique history and traditions – the Spurs Way and those glory glory nights – is a top-of-the-range special given a new sheen by the recent efforts of Poch and Levy on and off the field respectively. It was clear the club would be seeking a naming rights deal for the stadium, and would be hosting NFL games and other events. After just seven games at the stadium, a little more is known. There is no naming rights deal as yet, sponsors assessing a fully working stadium before thinking of committing. No other events have been staged at the stadium, and it is unclear if or how income from those other events will be used to underpin the football operation. But we do know that the restaurants and bars are doing a roaring trade, generating £800,000 at every game, according to *The Sun*. Every home game that went past at White Hart Lane saw Spurs fall another £1 million behind Arsenal.

Now in their spanking new home, their matchday income is likely to exceed that of their rivals (£3 million plus per home game). So the idea that stadium debt will be a burden is not as clear cut as the media like to portray, erroneously citing the plight of the neighbours down the road.

From a brand perspective and the long-term growth potential, the better strategy would be to emulate Manchester United rather than Arsenal. The Gunners took Emirates' money – a sponsor who had no previous connection to the club – and initially looked like tenants in their new home. United on the other hand have resisted the temptation from companies keen to associate themselves with Old Trafford, which as a result contributes a pure and powerful message to the United faithful as 'the theatre of dreams'.

Nevertheless, if Spurs believe that financial needs make it imperative to sponsor the stadium, then at least a compromise should be sought. Ideally, a prefix to the new White Hart Lane or the Tottenham Hotspur Stadium. Less cash certainly but at least only a junior partner will be taken on board which won't encroach too much on the intrinsic brand values. Over the years the Oval cricket ground has had many sponsors: the Fosters' Oval, the ANP Oval, the Brit Oval and the Kia Oval, but to Surrey members and the entire cricket world, it is still the Oval and always will be. Arsenal on the other hand, however much they have tried to put their stamp on their new home, still play at the home of an airline and always will until the sponsor has had enough.

It is unlikely that any English club will ever be able to challenge the omnipotence and omnipresence of Manchester United; the history of tragedy and triumph at home and abroad, domination in the Premier League era and the added bonus of Champions League wins have enabled them to withstand a fallow playing period since the departure of Sir Alex Ferguson and remain one of the richest clubs in the world. However, the competitive threat to United is now greater than it ever has been – Chelsea, Manchester City, Liverpool and now Spurs. As a consequence of their domestic and European success, Spurs have expanded their fan base to millions across the globe, and along with this their revenue and profit. At the end of the 2018 financial year (30 June) revenue stood at £380.7m and profit £113m, up from the previous year's figures of £309.7m and £36.2m. And both will certainly grow further when the exploits of 2019 are accounted for. Something special is going on in N17 and Enfield.

18

One Step from Glory

DURING THE last season at White Hart Lane, there was a togetherness that had not been seen for some years. The team's performances helped of course, but club and fans seemed to come together to see the old ground off, understanding each other's aspirations and providing mutual support in meeting them. It all culminated in a perfectly choreographed closing ceremony – featuring, among others, Sir Kenneth Branagh, the London Community Gospel Choir and tenor Wynne Evans – on 14 May 2017, in which a pitch invasion by thousands of fans held up the ceremony but which resulted in the most iconic image of the day as a rainbow appeared over the East Stand just as the delayed proceedings reached their conclusion.

The pitch invasion probably irritated some in the directors' box, who saw their carefully planned show put at risk by this spontaneous demonstration of affection. The fans, though, were determined to have their moment, and it turned out alright in the end. The club used the image of the rainbow to underline the emotion of that final day, accepting that there might still be a place for unplanned, raucous, spontaneous affection. A fitting epitaph for the old ground was presciently penned by Simon Inglis some years previously in his magnum opus *Football Grounds of Britain*, praising the Lane for 'its capacity for the unexpected. It was never refined. But unlike another club across North London, no one can say that life at White Hart Lane has ever been boring'.

Conceived with supporters in mind, the stands in the new ground are in close proximity to the pitch, with the *coup de grace* a striking single-tier home end with acoustics engineered to amplify the crowd noise. Once the stadium opened, the crowd gave themselves an integral role in the experience – as exemplified by the sight of hundreds of phones held aloft in the South Stand Market Place to film thousands of fellow fans singing songs and chanting, in order to post the footage online. Contemporary football culture feeding on itself.

However, the feeling remains that the club still views much of its relationship with its fans in transactional terms. It likes to say it has 'given' the fans a great stadium, but who is helping to pay for it? At present, satisfaction levels are high. However, if events take a turn for the worse there could be a backlash. The high price of everything from tickets to t-shirts, the reduction in the number of games on the season ticket, the lack of discount packages for Champions League group stage games... all this will fuel resentment. The real risk for the club is whether it can maintain its upward momentum. And this, despite the enormous strides made over the last few years, entails going further than it has up until now.

This is especially true because of the development of the Big Six league within a league, because the need for – and the ability of – that Big Six to retain their position grows stronger with every season. Unfortunately the corollary is that the Premier League becomes less and less competitive, its attractions reduced because fewer games really count, leaving the head-to-heads between the Big Six to determine to a large extent which one of them is going to walk off with the top prize. The broadcast companies, in turn, will cease to pay top dollar if their obligation is to televise every Premier League club a guaranteed number of times. Why, they will ask, should they pay £5m plus to televise Brighton v Bournemouth? For fans of the Big Six, the attraction of just being part of the exclusive club will wane if their team isn't a perennial contender. And the harsh reality is that Spurs, alone of all that group, have won neither of the modern game's two biggest prizes – the Premier League or the Champions League.

And so to the Spanish showdown, to an extraordinary occasion but – especially in light of the two semi-final second legs that preceded it – an anti-climactic end to an undreamed of, glorious journey. Nevertheless, the Spurs supporters admirably launched into a passionate chorus of *Oh When the Spurs Go Marching In* as the final whistle sounded. Their team had fallen one step short of the glory that would have changed so much for them, taken them into an elite band of clubs across the continent. A contentious early penalty call may have changed the way the night unfolded, Spurs may have looked the better of two lacklustre sides as the Spanish night became a dark journey into the soul for them, but while the pride remained and the regret dissipated in the hours, days and weeks that followed, the inevitable question repeatedly presented itself: did Poch mess up his selection and tactics for the biggest game of his, his players' and his supporters', lives?

Hindsight of course is a wonderful gift. All of us have 20:20 vision which enables us to be wise after the event. Was Poch's choice of his talisman, Harry Kane, a defining error that ensured Spurs ended up empty-handed, one step from glory? Kane had not played for seven weeks and hadn't scored for a month before that. From the outset, he appeared out of sorts, the effect contagious, the team a mirror image of him. Unimaginative, sluggish with no change of pace until the last frenetic minutes. Of course, had Lucas Moura started rather than Kane, there is no guarantee that the course of history would have been different. And if Kane, a truly world-class player, had not been selected to start when fit, questions would still have been asked. But Moura's speed and dynamism and that of Son, not played in a central role, was much missed. Moura arrived too late but in the last 25 minutes that he was given, he was more productive than Kane was in 90. Spurs had twice the amount of possession, made double the number of passes, but as had so often been the case during the second half of the Premier League campaign, the decision-making in the final third let them down. There was no end product when it mattered most.

After the game, Poch said: 'Today we'll begin to build Tottenham's future. Victories are built through pain and defeats.' Before the final he had intimated he may move on if he guided Spurs to victory – the sentiment seemingly that he would have achieved all he could with them. It was another of the manager's oddly timed comments, but now the indication was that he wanted to complete unfinished business. While some of a more fatalistic bent mused that this had been their team's one and only chance, the feeling that the chance would come again was not uncommon.

Put simply, the run to the Champions League Final disguised the fact that, in the Premier League, Spurs simply were not good enough during the second half of the season. In 18 games from 1 January to 12 May, Spurs took 26 points from a possible 54, winning just eight times. Five of those wins came before 23 February. So between 23 February and the end of the season, Spurs took just 11 points from a possible 36, beating only

Crystal Palace, already doomed Huddersfield Town, and narrow relegation escapees Brighton and Hove Albion. They finished the season 26 points behind their victorious opponents in Madrid.

The statistics – the cold, hard facts – measure the scale of progress yet to be made at home to match that already accomplished abroad. But football moves us because it is more than just a collection of numbers. And that is the reason why the story of a season in which a football club won nothing is, with apologies to Danny Blanchflower, so worthy of telling. It is the reason why, when the memories of the 2018/19 season are handed down, they will continue to burn brightly. Because despite all the reservations about modern football, the Spurs Champions League run stirred emotions, revived feelings many forgot they had and, above all, excited and inspired as never before.

Perhaps it is the contrasts that stand out the most, serving to sharpen the perspective and enhance the technicolour, surround sound, immersive sheer living of it all. From the depths of despair to the heights of ecstasy, each new twist and turn in the plot ramping up the emotions. And what a plot it was, packing in so many twists and turns that a brainstorming session at a

Hollywood scriptwriters' convention would find it too fanciful to contemplate.

Five times the adventure looked set to end, five times Spurs dragged themselves back in, each comeback more dramatic than the last. Harry Kane's two goals in 11 minutes against PSV Eindhoven in November to keep the team alive in a campaign that was, after just two minutes of that match, as good as over. Christian Eriksen's assured, surgical finish on 80 minutes in a must-win game against Inter Milan to keep the possibility of qualification open. Lucas Moura's late, late strike at the Nou Camp to take the Lilywhites into the knockout stages by the most implausible of routes. Fernando Llorente blowing off the cobwebs in a helter-skelter version of next-goal-wins-it on a passionate, crazy night in Manchester to score the goal that did, then didn't, then did take Spurs to the semi-final when all had seemed lost so many, many times. Moura again in Amsterdam on that night of nights, darting in between two Ajax defenders to swipe a ball through the narrowest of gaps and into the corner of the net to complete a second-half hat-trick that turned the world upside down; the vital away goal coming six minutes into added time after Spurs had been three goals down on aggregate with three-quarters of the tie played.

The stuff of legend, the scenario almost impossible to conceive, leaving those who watched from the stands physically drained but able to run on pure adrenalin to celebrate the moment. Transfixed in the floodlit bowl by the actors weaving their story on the big green stage, as the compelling events unfolded before their eyes, the intoxicating atmosphere the fans generated gave them an intrinsic role in the drama like vast numbers of extras on a film set. Football, it is often forgotten, is entertainment and on nights like these there is nothing to match it.

These nights, many fans said, are what we do it for. All the past disappointment and dismay cast aside in an instant. Pride and passion burst forth, revelling in being at the centre of the universe. To dare and to do, to not just win but to win in style.

Characters are key in any great drama and this epic was blessed with some absorbing storylines. Goalkeeper Hugo Lloris found redemption after a drink-driving conviction in the early days of the season and some unsteady performances including a red card in Eindhoven led some to question if his day had gone. Left-back Danny Rose overcame challenging personal issues and lingering resentment over his criticism of the club to become a figure revered not just for his passion and ability on the pitch, but his courage off it. Son Heung-min established himself as a leader of the line, no longer just considered an understudy or a foil for Harry Kane. As for Kane himself, a curate's egg of a season. Not his best one by any means, as injury and fatigue – both physical and mental – appeared to have taken its toll on him. But he still struck at vital moments, remained a source of inspiration and was at the centre of some of the key events in the story. As was Christian Eriksen, who along with Kane was the only other undisputed world-class player in the ranks.

Moussa Sissoko, once a derided figure, now bestrode the midfield like a colossus, every inch a France international, breaking up opposition attacks and carrying the ball forward. Another who moved to centre stage as the campaign unfolded was Lucas Moura. He had seemed to be one of those imports who were fated to never quite fit in. But the vital goals at the Nou Camp and, of course, in Amsterdam gave the lie to that impression. Toby Alderweireld and Jan Vertonghen showed there were no ill effects from their World Cup exploits and their steadfastness and versatility constantly bolstered the defence. Similar qualities were consistently displayed by young Harry Winks and spasmodically by Érik Lamela and Dele Alli who, although a star below par, shone brightly on occasions. Kieran Trippier, short of his best, showed his worth from time to time as did Eric Dier, Victor Wanyama, Serge Aurier, Ben Davis and Davinson Sánchez when called upon.

Finally and arguably the most unlikely tale of all, one Fernando Llorente. Seemingly another misfit striker to stir uncomfortable memories of Sergei Rebrov, Roberto Soldado and numerous others, Llorente made his point briefly and decisively. Destined for a minor role, he emerged as a central character in the later stages of the campaign, scoring against Borussia Dortmund just three minutes after arriving as a substitute, bagging the decisive goal on that manic night in Manchester and then turning in a pivotal performance in the Miracle of Amsterdam. The sight of the tall Spaniard, mouth wide, neck muscles tensed, arms outstretched as he ran to the crowd after scoring against Manchester City will remain one of the iconic images for Spurs fans for years to come.

The season was memorable in large part because the fans lived vicariously, joyously alongside their heroes as the exploits they created one after another enabled them to savour the experience much as a good drama serial is perhaps better appreciated week by week than in a box-set binge. Good things come to those who wait.

'One of the features of Pochettino's time at Spurs,' says Alan Fisher, whose *Tottenham On My Mind* blog so often distils the essence of fan feeling, 'is how he and his players have created a close relationship with the fans.' Nowhere was this more apparent than when, in the Johan Cruyff Arena, Spurs knew they were just one step from glory. Fisher expresses it perfectly when he says, 'Pochettino's tears established an unbreakable bond between him and the supporters. He has always understood what our heritage means for us. Now, he is one of us, overwhelmed with the joy of being Spurs. That reaction was about us, not personal reputation. Pochettino gives us the words to express our feelings about the club in a way matched only by the illustrious Bill Nicholson. Bill wanted to aim high, for players to give their all for the fans. Tottenham was his life and he loved the club. Pochettino, in his moment of triumph, also digs deep: "Without football, it is impossible to live." Modestly, he thanked his players for being "heroes", but here is a man who understands what this victory, this club, means to everybody who reveres the navy blue and white. Football is life itself. This win makes us truly alive. We feel the blood pulsing in our veins, sensations are heightened, life and love is better than it was before. We reach deep down into our heart and soul to find out something about who we are, what matters, and who we can be. Only football can do this for us. Poch knows.'

He also knows how to adjust to the tempo of the moment chameleon-like – someone who wants to sign players early but who is also content not to sign stars, who wants to develop youth, who is in *de facto* charge of the playing side but who is frustrated that his ambitions might not be fulfilled. He plays his cards well, managing to avoid the factionalism of his predecessors and staying onside with a board that has been known to take umbrage if it feels slighted.

In December 2017, Poch sent what was widely interpreted as a coded message to his boss. 'We are going to try again to do it early,' he said in answer to a question about bringing in reinforcements. The Chairman was well known for his brinkmanship, which had served Spurs so well both in buying and selling. Yet, the following two transfer windows opened and closed with no action whatsoever. Spurs were the only club in

Europe's top five leagues to not sign anyone, and the first Premier League club to make no new signings in a transfer window since it came into play in 2002/03. The subsequent explanation was that Poch hadn't wanted anyone. And he was happy to go along with it.

And yet the tide of time rolls on. Speaking to Spanish newspaper *Marca* in June 2019, Poch had changed his tune, stating: 'It is essential this year that the team is reinforced.' He went on to explain why he might not get his wish. 'In Manchester City and Liverpool, Pep Guardiola and Jürgen Klopp are free to decide which players they want and what they do not. On the other hand, in other teams such as Tottenham, Chelsea or Arsenal it is not in the hands of trainers. Who decides, in our case, is the President.'

Alan Fisher linked Poch to Bill Nick, the club's most successful manager. Arguably the line began even further back with Arthur Rowe. After all, it was Rowe who persuaded the great Danny Blanchflower to come to Spurs from Aston Villa in 1954, convincing him to turn down overtures from Arsenal, who were at the time the more successful and richer club. Blanchflower had been impressed by Rowe's 1951 league title-winning side, and subsequently explained his choice, 'I was convinced that their [Spurs'] style of play was more in keeping with the future than Arsenal's.'

Poch's way is, in many respects, the Spurs Way. He has fashioned his own version for modern times, reminding Spurs and their fans of what constitutes success in the modern game. Rewarding their loyalty and fulfilling their dreams, he's not been afraid to ruffle feathers to do so, but has never been judged to have overstepped the mark as some did before him. He has rid the club of its reputation for being pushovers, and no longer can opposition managers patronisingly exhort their players 'Come on lads, it's only Spurs'. The taunts about Spurs always falling at the final hurdle ignore the fact that, for generations, they got nowhere near the ultimate challenge. That is a measure of Poch's achievement.

A Champions League Final is always a watershed, and yet it is safe to say the final of 2019 was one of the least memorable. After the trials and tribulations both contestants had to overcome on their epic journeys to Madrid, perhaps it was inevitable that the end of the campaign would be an anti-climax. Nonetheless, the measure of what had been achieved was in the fact that the thought of Spurs getting another shot at winning 'the one with the big ears' was not totally outlandish. Perhaps even more importantly, the players felt they were contenders, illustrating that Poch's belief that victories can be forged in the fires of defeat may have some future veracity.

A campaign of such contortions, such high drama and emotion seared into the consciousness, is done a disservice by being viewed simply through the prism of what might have been. It will be recalled as a pure, life-affirming, crazy journey. It took fans somewhere new, somewhere they had never been before and had been told over and over again was a mere pipe-dream. That's why this ultimately unsuccessful campaign will be cherished for ever and a day. As co-chair of the Tottenham Hotspur Supporters' Trust, Katrina Law, said, some weeks after the warmth of the Madrid sun had conceded to the half-hearted humidity of London, 'If I could do it all again knowing how it would turn out, I would in a heartbeat.'

Sometimes a Champions League Final signals an end of an era, the last throes of a team which has reached its peak and is about to be dismantled. For others it is the first sight of the promised land. Will Poch, like Moses, have to reconcile himself to the fact that the vista is as close as he will ever get? Or will he be able to rise to the challenge, domestic if not European, and take his men that one step further to glory?

Postscript: New Steps to Glory?

'IF WE want to win titles we need to operate in a different way.' Those were Poch's words in January 2019, before the extraordinary story of the season had played out. By August and the close of the transfer window, the club showed it was prepared to do so. Spending of over £100m, with possible further millions in settlement of structured deals, made Spurs the sixth-biggest Premier League net spenders in the summer transfer window with over £60m.

Players purchased were 22-year-old Tanguy Ndombélé from Lyon, one of the most highly rated midfield talents in Europe, for an initial £54m – a club record fee. Promising 18-year-old winger Jack Clarke was signed from Leeds for £9m plus in a deal that could see the fee rise to over £10m and immediately loaned back to the Championship club. With these purchases completed in early July, the club seemed to be addressing a number of the criticisms regularly levelled at it. It had moved early and decisively, it had spent big, and it had backed the manager.

Then, like the summer in which an extended heatwave threatened but never quite materialised, the momentum faltered. The narrative began to take on a familiar tone. Spurs were publicly linked with a number of potential acquisitions, but apparently negotiations were running into trouble over the price, the structure, the detail. Familiar questions began to surface. Was the club really going to back the manager all the way? Would it break the habit and end up with a considerable net spend or were the links with big names just a ruse to appease the fans? In the frenetic atmosphere of the modern game's manufactured transfer window drama, it can be difficult to work out who is spinning who and to what purpose.

Nerves were frayed further by another of Poch's enigmatic interventions. At the end of July, in a media conference on the club's tour of Singapore, he responded testily to questions on transfers by saying: 'I am not in charge and I know nothing about the situation of my players. I am only coaching them and trying to get the best from them. Sell, buy players, sign contract, not sign contract – I think it is not in my hands, it's in the club's hands and Daniel Levy… Today I feel like I am the coach' [i.e. not the manager].

The picture painted contrasted sharply with that presented by the club the previous October when, amid criticism of the lack of activity on transfers, the intimation was that Poch had not wanted to bring anyone in.

In the end, it all came down to deadline day, 8 August 2019, which Spurs ended by signing Giovani Lo Celso from Real Betis, another highly rated midfielder who Poch had made clear was a prime target. After protracted negotiations, the 23-year-old was signed in the kind of smart deal that exemplifies Spurs' transfer strategy – an initial £15m fee with an obligation to purchase after one season, and an outstanding £40m to be paid then. The structure enabled Betis to reduce the fees that needed to be paid to Lo Celso's previous clubs while easing the immediate pressure on Spurs' finances.

Much excitement had been generated over the possible arrival of Juventus' Argentinian international Paulo Dybala, one of Europe's most highly rated forwards. On the surface, this seemed to be the very opposite of the kind of deal Spurs favoured. A player demanding, it was reported, an astronomical sum in wages, an agent wanting a huge cut, and a third-party owner of image rights also to be accounted for. Even so, reliable sources say the club was definitely interested and was working on a deal for some time until it became clear, just hours before the deadline, that it was futile. If it had come off, alongside the other signings, it would have been sensational. It was a shame that the turmoil eclipsed news of the club's final signing of the window, long-time target Ryan Sessegnon, Fulham's coveted 19-year-old left-sided starlet, another player Poch had made it known he wanted, and just the type who he has a reputation for transforming from good to great.

With full-back Kieran Trippier leaving for Atlético Madrid for £20m and the forward Vincent Janssen offloaded to Monterrey in Mexico for £8m, this brought the net spend to more than £60m. No one could now say that the board was not backing the manager – three players he had made clear were his top targets had been secured. And the criticism that Spurs never took the chance to move on could be firmly dismissed.

With the transfer window still open in Italy, Spain, Germany and France till 2 September. following the English Premier League's unfathomable decision to close earlier than their competitors, there is still a chance that Spurs could see more players go, with the talented playmaker Christian Eriksen clearly signalling he wants a move. Losing a player of Eriksen's ability – 49 goals and 60 assists in 206 Premier League appearances in a Spurs shirt – can never be a positive outcome, but with a year left on his contract and his heart seemingly not in N17, a sale may be the best practical solution all round.

The new recruits indicate Poch may be planning to change his *modus operandi*; less reliance on full-backs – an area where the squad remains light – and with options in midfield greatly increased by the new acquisitions. Midfield in particular is fascinating, with a raft of players able to take on multiple roles, and most under 23 years old. After changing the way they do business off the field while largely staying true to their principles, Spurs may be about to do the same on the pitch.

The last word goes to Poch, who said this on the eve of the new season. 'You learn after defeats. You learn after victories. You learn after finals. You begin to move on, to refresh yourself, and of course we have the motivation and the challenge to do an amazing season again.'